C000141033

THE FA CUP
Miscellany

THE FA CUP
Miscellany

*Trivia, History, Facts & Stats
from Football's Most Famous Cup*

MICHAEL KEANE

THE FA CUP
Miscellany

© Michael Keane

Michael Keane has asserted his rights in accordance with the Copyright, Designs and Patents Act 1988 to be identified as the author of this work.

Published By:
Pitch Publishing (Brighton) Ltd
A2 Yeoman Gate
Yeoman Way
Durrington
BN13 3QZ

Email: info@pitchpublishing.co.uk
Web: www.pitchpublishing.co.uk

First published 2013

All rights reserved. No part of this publication may be reproduced, stored in a retrieval system, or transmitted in any form or by any means, electronic, mechanical, photocopying, recording or otherwise, without the prior permission in writing of the publisher and the copyright owners.

A catalogue record for this book is available from the British Library.

13-digit ISBN: 978-1-9091784-8-9

Typesetting and origination by Pitch Publishing.

Printed and bound by CPI Group (UK) Ltd, Croydon, CR0 4YY

This book is dedicated to Gabby,
Thomas, Oliver, Patrick
and Annabelle, who remain
my favourite team.

FOREWORD BY DAVE BEASANT

I was fortunate enough to enjoy a fantastic playing career spanning four decades, I came through the non-league route and ended up playing for close to 20 years at the top level of the game in this country, I was capped by England during Bobby Robson's reign as boss and was part of the Three Lions squad that went to Italia 90 - but the one standout memory from my playing days is winning the FA Cup with Wimbledon in 1988.

It was every football-loving schoolboy's dream to lead their team out in the FA Cup Final as captain, and I was no different when I was working towards making it as a professional footballer with Edgeware Town in the late 1970s. I eventually got my break into the pro game in 1979, when Wimbledon, then in the old Third Division put their faith in me as a 20-year-old, but having stepped up to full-time football, never in my wildest dreams did I envisage that one day I would be leading out the Crazy Gang in the May sunshine beneath those famous Wembley twin towers... and neither did I think I'd be saving a penalty against one of the greatest club sides in the world, to help us pull off one of the greatest Cup Final shocks of all time. We went to Wembley with everyone outside of Wimbledon expecting us to make up the numbers against league champions Liverpool. As crazy as it might sound, we fancied our chances and Lawrie Sanchez's winning goal meant we came home with the FA Cup!

That's just my story – it still makes the hair on the back of my neck stand on end, every time I tell it. There are so many romantic tales from the game's oldest and most-famous cup competition, and you will find plenty of those stories and anecdotes in *The FA Cup Miscellany*. The competition may have evolved, just as the game has over the years, but the FA Cup will always have its own special magic, and it's celebrated in the pages of this book.

ACKNOWLEDGEMENTS

Thanks are due to several people who have helped me put this book together. From the last 12 months, thanks to Pitch Publishing for giving me the opportunity to write this book, and particular thanks to Paul Camillin, Gareth Davis and Dave Beasant. A huge thank-you is also due to my family for their encouragement, their patience and their support. Lastly, I want to thank the players, the teams and even the managers who have taken part in football's longest running, and best competition; for its drama and its unpredictability, the FA Cup stands apart.

INTRODUCTION

The FA Cup Miscellany covers over 140 years of fantastic knockout football. Throughout all that time, the oldest and simplest domestic cup competition in the world has provided spectators with a glut of great entertainment and many memories to treasure.

There have been games with terrific twists and turns; there have been players who were villains and players who were heroes; for the many millions of fans who have followed the FA Cup there has also been the great fun of watching the stories unfold. All sorts of FA Cup-related stories, facts and figures are included here. Those memorable upsets are mentioned; from the great Wembley shocks of Sunderland and Southampton's victories, to Sutton United's humbling of then-First Division Coventry City.

Great players are covered; from Stanley Matthews' wing wizardry in 1953 to Steven Gerrard's Millennium masterclass of 2006. Great stories are also included; from the day a 20-stone, naked goalkeeper chased a referee into a broom cupboard, to the time when a Teletext page catapulted Wycombe to a semi-final.

By writing this collection of FA Cup tales I hope to gently jog readers' memories of many cup highlights, and to share my enthusiasm for the best unscripted drama that you can find – the surprising, the dramatic and the glorious, game of football. As Danny Blanchflower once famously said, 'the game is about glory' and I hope this book proves it.

Michael Keane

EARLY DAYS

When the FA Cup was first contested, in the 1871/72 season, the competition was unrecognisable from the national landmark it has since become. Only the following 15 teams took part in the inaugural event: Clapham Rovers; Upton Park; Crystal Palace; Hitchin; Maidenhead; Great Marlow; Barnes; Civil Service; Wanderers; Harrow Chequers; Royal Engineers; Reigate Priory; Queen's Park; Donnington School; Hampstead Heathens. The first winners of the trophy, Wanderers, enjoyed an unconventional route to cup success. In the first round Wanderers' opponents, Harrow Chequers, scratched, so next up was a second round tie with Clapham Rovers. Wanderers beat Clapham 3-1 and then drew with Crystal Palace in the quarter-final before both teams were allowed into the semi-final. There had been an odd number of teams in the quarter-finals so Queen's Park were given a bye, then Wanderers and Palace were allowed through to make up the numbers. Scotland's Queen's Park drew 0-0 with Wanderers in the semi-final, but then had to withdraw from the competition as they could not afford to travel back to London for a replay, allowing Wanderers to play in the final against Royal Engineers. Wanderers famously won the first FA Cup Final 1-0 thanks to a goal from Morton Betts. The 2,000 spectators at the Kennington Oval might not have thought it then, but they had witnessed the birth of the most prestigious domestic cup competition in the world.

SIX AND OUT!

Denis Law almost rewrote the FA Cup record books when he played for Manchester City in the fourth round at Luton Town in January 1961. Law scored all six of City's goals as the Maine Road men ran riot. Sadly for Law, as the goals rained in the heavens opened and the pitch was fast becoming unplayable. With barely 20 minutes left the ground was so waterlogged the referee abandoned the match and the result was not allowed to stand. Just days later the hastily rearranged fixture was replayed and while Law added another to his tally, this time the Second Division Hatters sprang an upset and won 3-1. Had Law's six goals stood he would have sat at the top of the all-time FA Cup scorers list, clear of Ian Rush's subsequent record. In later years Law remained modest about his deeds, declaring simply: "It's not every day that you score six goals." He might have added: "And lose"!

THE FA CUP FINAL SINGLE: SPURS WITH CHAS N DAVE RECORD THEIR 1991 FINAL RECORD

THE THINGS THEY SAY 1

"It is desirable that a Challenge Cup shall be established in connection with the Association." Charles Alcock, secretary of the FA, explaining the new competition in 1871.

"If there's a goal scored now, I'll eat my hat." Commentating on the first televised final in 1938, Thomas Woodrooffe had clearly given up on seeing a goal after nearly 120 goalless minutes. Moments later Preston were awarded a last-minute penalty which they scored to win the match. Reports suggest Woodrooffe went on to eat a hat-shaped cake to atone for his gaffe!

"The great match of the year." A MovieTone News 1952 broadcast describing that year's final between Newcastle United and Arsenal.

"I've won a championship medal, a European medal and countless Scotland caps, but sometimes I think I'd swap the lot for an FA Cup winners' medal." Leeds United captain Billy Bremner, before the 1972 final against Arsenal.

"But wait a moment." ITV commentator Brian Moore reacts as Graham Rix's last-minute cross is missed by Manchester United's Gary Bailey, allowing Arsenal's Alan Sunderland to sneak a dramatic winner.

GETTING SHIRTY

The 1987 FA Cup Final between Coventry City and Tottenham Hotspur is remembered for many things: Houchen's flying header; Coventry's first major trophy; and perhaps even the sight of managers Sillett and Curtis dancing in tandem on the pitch. However, a close inspection of the footage of the game reveals something else unusual and unprecedented. As Tottenham graced the Wembley turf that day, someone, somewhere behind the scenes had got into a tangle with their team strip. Instead of all 11 players walking out resplendent in their shiny white Hummel shirts, emblazoned with the sponsor's name, Holsten, astride their chests, six players went out wearing shirts without a sponsor's name on them at all. In the increasingly corporate-conscious football world of the late 1980s, such an omission was unacceptable. As if David Pleat had not suffered enough in watching his side's surprise defeat, on the Monday after the match he had to meet with officials from the German brewers Holsten to try and explain the mix-up. What Pleat made of that meeting is unrecorded, but it is fair to assume his concerns on Cup Final day were less to do with the laundry and a little more to do with the picking up of a cup!

WHAT'S IN A NAME?

The FA Cup is an all-embracing and far-reaching competition which is played the length and breadth of the country. Not all the teams in it are household names though; for every Rovers, United or City, there are plenty of other teams whose titles might raise an eyebrow. The Evo-Stik Northern Premier League Premier Division includes one of the most famous non-league names – Blyth Spartans, who almost made the quarter-finals in 1978. Spartans have been going since 1899, and took their name from a club secretary who clearly knew his classical references; he thought the club should try to emulate the feared battlers of the Greek Spartan army. The Northern League Division One is also host to some clubs with memorable names. Bedlington Terriers play there and must be one of the few clubs to include the name of a dog in their title. Terriers' rivals include Billingham Synthonia, who take their name from an old ICI product – synthetic ammonia – a synthetic fertiliser! Another stand-out name from the north is Norton & Stockton Ancients who play in the same division. The Ancients are an amalgamation of two separate clubs, Norton and Stockton, who merged in 1980, with the Ancients suffix added to provide some continuity with their past. While Leicestershire is a fine part of the world, not everyone might know that it boasts a blissful haven of release, a nirvana of its own – Thurnby Nirvana of the East Midlands Counties League. It is just four years since the club was formed, after Thurnby Rangers and Leicester Nirvana merged and though currently at step six of the non-league pyramid, the club website states that they soon hope to be "knocking on the door of the Football League", before finishing with a sentiment that football fans of any level can relate to: "The beauty of football and the reason we all love it is, you never know!"

TROUBLE WITH THE NEIGHBOURS

Rumour has it that when Derby County moved into the Baseball Ground in 1895, they upset one or two of their neighbours. Derby's new home was partly built on land where some gypsies had been staying and the construction of a new football ground did not go down well. The travellers were moved on, as professional football put down roots in Derby. According to legend, the aggrieved gypsies put a curse on Derby to stop them winning any trophies, as revenge for their ejection. When Derby reached, and then lost, three FA Cup Finals between 1898 and 1903, the rumours of the curse seemed more believable. Although the Rams did enjoy some success over the next four decades – three promotions were gained from the Second Division – it was not until 1946 that they reached another Cup Final. Prior to lining up against Charlton at Wembley, it is said that representatives of the club were so worried about the story that they sought out descendants of the original gypsy families to try to end the curse. Although it is hard to verify exactly what was said and by whom, the facts of the match speak for themselves; after extra-time was needed, Derby won an absorbing final 4-1. Superstitious types have suggested the exact moment the curse was lifted was when Derby shot for goal in the dying minutes only for the ball to burst in mid-air. We will never know for sure whether Derby's win had more to do with Jackie Stamps' double in the extra period, or the benevolence of some gypsies lifting their curse. What we can say for certain though, is that when the Rams moved again, in 1997 to Pride Park, this time they made sure there were no groups of travellers on nearby land!

HAVE WE MET BEFORE? 1

Over the years, some Cup Final pairings have been repeated more than any other. In the competition's early days, Midlands rivals Aston Villa and West Bromwich Albion got to know each other very well after three finals in eight years.

1887 – Aston Villa 2 West Bromwich Albion 0
1892 – Aston Villa 0 West Bromwich Albion 3
1895 – Aston Villa 1 West Bromwich Albion 0

These early finals reflected strength in Midlands football that has seldom been approached since. Three times in eight years West Brom and Villa faced each other, twice at Kennington Oval and lastly at Crystal Palace. Both teams had a win each when they met for the third time, but it was Villa who famously won, and then lost, the trophy in 1895. The ball which West Brom put into the Villa net three times in 1892 was auctioned earlier in 2012 for £15,000.

JOE HARVEY, CAPTAIN OF 1951 WINNERS NEWCASTLE UNITED, LIFTS THE CUP AT WEMBLEY

THE MAGNIFICENT SEVEN

If England left-back Ashley Cole ever decides to forge a new career in management, one thing he won't have to worry about is his players doubting his credentials. At the time of writing, Cole's medal collection, accumulated over more than a decade for Arsenal and Chelsea, is nothing short of fantastic. He has won league titles, a Champions League and he has also won more FA Cup Finals than anyone else in the 140-year history of the competition – seven in total. Though Cole's triumphs have coincided with the Premiership era of elite clubs dominating every domestic competition, that Cole has figured in seven finals and won them all is impressive. It is worth noting that in all the finals in which Cole has played, his two sides have conceded just twice; testament to his defensive qualities. Cole's seven finals are: 2001/02 Arsenal 2 Chelsea 0; 2002/03 Arsenal 1 Southampton 0; 2004/05 Arsenal 0 Manchester United 0 (Arsenal won 5-4 on penalties); 2006/07 Chelsea 1 Manchester United 0; 2008/09 Chelsea 2 Everton 1; 2009/10 Chelsea 1 Portsmouth 0; 2011/12 Chelsea 2 Liverpool 1.

ON THE SPOT

What could easily have been a long-forgotten quarter-final in 1890/91 between Notts County and Stoke City has gone down in footballing history as being a pivotal moment in the development of the laws of the game. In the same way that at the last World Cup Luis Suarez prevented a certain Ghana goal by pushing the ball out with his hands, County defender Hendry did exactly the same thing. The ball was already past his keeper when Hendry punched it off the line to deny Stoke a certain goal. In the days before penalties, this gave the referee a major problem; the best he could do was award Stoke a free kick on the goal-line. The attempted shot was instantly gathered by the County keeper and when Stoke went on to lose 1-0, their sense of injustice was unrivalled. The match and that incident provoked lots of debate about what should and should not have happened. The idea that, in effect, cheating had been rewarded sat uncomfortably with football administrators and fans alike. By the start of the following season the laws of the game were changed to include, for the first time, the award of a penalty for serious infringements.

SEEING RED

Over decades, the FA Cup has become synonymous with many things; full-blooded contests; dramatic climaxes; the passionate nature of its matches continuing to draw great crowds. In January 1979, all those things came together in a third round tie between Second Division side Charlton Athletic and Alliance Premier outfit Maidstone United. With time running out, Charlton were being held 1-1 by their non-league opponents and frustration was in the air. It was soon on the pitch too as a Charlton break ended with Derek Hales being flagged offside. Hales was not best pleased and he lost his cool, in spectacular fashion. Hales did not vent his fury at the linesman who had thwarted him or the referee who had whistled; instead when he saw team-mate Mike Flanagan, he decided his very own strike partner was the man to blame for not passing a moment earlier. Rather than gesticulate or simply holler instructions, Hales thought he needed to make his point in a quick yet forceful manner so, when the pair approached each other, Hales smartly punched his team-mate. Astonished spectators and players alike looked on as Charlton's attackers quickly exchanged punches rather than passes, leaving the referee little option but to send them both off. While Hales and Flanagan went down in FA Cup folklore for their flurry of fists, Charlton's other nine men held out for a draw before going on to win the replay.

OFF THE SADDLE

When Arsenal were drawn away to Walsall in the third round in 1933, a local leather shopkeeper started to do some sums. He calculated that the £87 Arsenal had spent on their boots that year was worth remembering as it contrasted neatly with the £70 Walsall had been able to spend on their entire team; it was to be a contest between the haves and the have-nots. The Gunners had reached two Cup Finals in four years, and were about to win their second league championship in three years just months later. In that same time Walsall had been scratching around the lower reaches of the Third Division, both North and South, and nothing seemed to suggest an upset was possible. The respective status of each side counted for little though when kick-off arrived, as Walsall ploughed immediately into their more illustrious opponents with some rustic challenges. The game remained goalless for an hour until Gilbert

Alsop's header put the Saddlers in front and they went on to double their lead from the penalty spot when Bill Sheppard scored after being fouled by debutant Tommy Black. The Fellows Park crowd, some of whom encroached on to the pitch, went delirious as the unbelievable unfurled in front of them, while Arsenal manager Herbert Chapman was so furious afterwards he banned Black from Highbury and the defender never played for Arsenal again.

DID YOU KNOW?

There have been 42 different winners of the FA Cup. Manchester United lead the way with 11 triumphs, closely followed by Arsenal on ten with Tottenham Hotspur third on eight. Liverpool and Aston Villa are tied with seven, as are three teams with six – Newcastle United, Chelsea and Blackburn Rovers, and a further four teams on five – Everton, West Bromwich Albion, Manchester City and Wanderers. Three teams have four wins – Wolverhampton Wanderers, Bolton Wanderers and Sheffield United, and the Blades' rivals Sheffield Wednesday are one of two teams with three wins alongside West Ham United. Preston North End, Old Etonians, Portsmouth, Sunderland, Nottingham Forest and Bury are the clubs to have won the FA Cup twice, and there is also a long list of those to have won it just once. Huddersfield Town, Southampton, Leeds United, Derby County, Royal Engineers, Oxford University, Blackpool, Cardiff City, Burnley, Charlton Athletic, Barnsley, Notts County, Clapham Rovers, Wimbledon, Coventry City, Ipswich Town, Bradford City, Blackburn Olympic and Old Carthusians all have one FA Cup triumph to their name.

HITMAN HARRY

In 140 years of the FA Cup no-one has scored more goals than Harry Cursham, a Notts County striker of the 1870s and 80s. Although Cursham is credited with 49 strikes in total, he was never an FA Cup winner at Meadow Lane, as he did not play in the Magpies' triumph of 1891. Cursham could play on either side of the pitch and his eye for goal continued onto the international arena, playing eight times for England between 1882 and 1884, and scoring a very healthy five goals. Cursham also played in two first-class cricket matches for Nottinghamshire, which, bizarrely, were some 24 years apart!

THE GREATEST WEMBLEY FA CUP GOAL? GAZZA'S STUNNING FREE KICK AGAINST ARSENAL IN THE 1991 SEMI-FINAL, THE FIRST YEAR THEY WERE PLAYED AT WEMBLEY

RIPPING UP THE FORMBOOK 1

In nearly 70 years since the end of the war, only six times have non-league teams knocked top flight (First Division and Premiership) sides out of the FA Cup. Here are the first three occasions with the remaining three to follow later:

1947/48 Third round, Colchester United (Southern League) 1 Huddersfield Town 0: Layer Road witnessed the first occasion that a non-league side knocked out a First Division team. After watching Huddersfield play, Colchester manager Ted Fenton declared he had a plan to beat his first division opponents and what became known as the "F-Plan" worked. Colchester went on to reach the fifth round for the first time in their history, where they lost to Stanley Matthews' Wembley-bound Blackpool.

1948/49 Fourth round, Yeovil Town (Southern League) 2 Sunderland 1: Sunderland boasted the most expensive British player of the time in £20,500 striker Len Shackleton, and were regarded as one of the wealthiest clubs in the country. The contrast with the amateurs of Yeovil with their sloping pitch could not have been greater, but resources counted for nothing as Yeovil famously won in extra time. Yeovil player-manager Alec Stock, scorer of the first goal, had his players on a strength-building diet of eggs, sherry and glucose which clearly did them no harm!

1971/72 Third round, Hereford United (Southern League) 2 Newcastle United 1: The game that has since become immortalised by countless BBC replays of Ronnie Radford's goal was classic cup-tie fare. All the ingredients were there: a David v Goliath tie, a virtually unplayable muddy pitch and an unbelievable result – what has long been regarded as the magic of the FA Cup was very much in evidence at Edgar Street.

THE TOP AND BOTTOM OF IT

George Graham's Arsenal teams of the 1980s and 90s were renowned for many things; they were resolute; they were experts of the 1-0 victory and they were winners. As the Arsenal team bus arrived at Wrexham's Racecourse Ground in January 1992 for an FA Cup third round tie, few people could have looked beyond the men from Highbury securing their passage into the next round of the competition at the expense of the struggling Welsh outfit. The cup draw had certainly worked its magic in pairing the teams together. Arsenal were defending Football League champions, officially the best team in the country; Wrexham had finished at the very bottom of the league, 24th out of 24 in the fourth tier; officially the worst team in the country. It looked about as monumental a mismatch as you could hope to find – aristocrats versus artisans. The first half followed a well trodden script with Alan Smith poaching a goal and Arsenal's back four of Lee Dixon, Nigel Winterburn, Tony Adams and David O'Leary looking impenetrable in front of David Seaman. With just eight minutes left the headline writers seemed in for an easy evening, with another routine 1-0 win for Arsenal unfolding. It was then that veteran defender O'Leary tangled with Gordon Davies on the edge of the Arsenal penalty area and conceded a direct free kick. Fellow old-stager Mickey Thomas, a still sprightly 37, placed the ball down and simply belted it into the top corner of Seaman's net; taking a free kick never looked easier. Two minutes later O'Leary and Adams failed to prevent or clear a left-wing cross and young striker Steve Watkin fired home from the six-yard line. In just three minutes the football pyramid had been turned on its axis and Arsenal were dumped out of the cup. For Mickey Thomas it was a kind of revenge on Arsenal, having lost the dramatic 1979 final against them when playing for Manchester United. His joy was short-lived however as within days he was making altogether different headlines for his involvement in a counterfeiting scam. Thomas's fall from grace was as dramatic as anything he could conjure up on the football field and he served time in Walton Prison. It was Thomas the footballer though who had the ability to make all the right headlines on the pitch; as Wrexham fans know, when he was on song he could charm a football to do anything he wanted it to.

MASTER CLASS

In February 1970, Fourth Division side Northampton Town landed the plum draw of that year's fifth round, a home tie with Manchester United. The Cobblers would be hosting a United team that not two years earlier had won the European Cup, and though struggling to maintain those dizzy heights, United still boasted some stellar names like Bobby Charlton, Brian Kidd and George Best. In the build-up to the match, Northampton fans would have hoped and maybe even dreamed of an unlikely upset; United were not the team they had been and, perhaps, if Town had a bucketful of good luck and United had an off-day, a shock could happen. Thoughts of a cup shock storyline increased in the days before the game as there was uncertainty as to whether United's top star, George Best, would actually play. Best had been suspended for the previous four matches and was unlikely to be match-fit. However, Northampton's optimism was deflated shortly before kick-off when the United team-sheet confirmed Best's appearance; after a month off centre-stage the great entertainer was back, and he had some catching up to do. Talk of an upset was muted each time Best touched the ball as he immediately rampaged around the boggy surface; defenders were glued to the pitch while the ball was glued to Best's feet. Best scored twice in the first half, a far-post header and smart sidestep past the keeper, but this was just the warm-up for the main action of the afternoon. After the interval, a scrambled goal, another header and then a cool finish gave the striker five goals, but he was not finished there. Best's coup de grace was the goal of the game. Picking up a Paddy Crerand through ball, he seemed to dummy the goalkeeper Kim Book in slow motion, leaving Book grounded before rolling home his sixth of the afternoon. Best's feat leaves him as the only United player to score six in a match since before the First World War and to commemorate his achievement Northampton's players gave him a signed match ball. While the romance of an upset was not seen at the County Ground that day, Best's love affair with football was evident to everyone. He was a man who could do anything with the ball and when he was on song defenders had no answer to his twists and turns; trying to stop Best in full flight was like trying to catch the wind.

ABIDE WITH ME

Since 1927, an essential part of FA Cup Final day has been the singing of the hymn *Abide with Me* before kick-off. Football fans of all teams have come to recognise the hymn as signalling the start of the domestic game's showpiece occasion and the imminent ending of the football season. It is still debated if the then-reigning monarch, King George V, requested *Abide With Me* be included in the pre-match ritual, or whether one of his favourite hymns was inserted

THE F.A. CUP SPONSORED BY AXA

WINNERS 2000

AXA

CHELSEA WERE THE LAST WINNERS AT WEMBLEY BEFORE THE TWIN TOWERS CAME DOWN AND THE FAMOUS STADIUM WAS REBUILT

by the FA for his benefit. Either way, the hymn quickly became as much a part of Cup Final routine as the captain's joyful raising of the old trophy itself. The words to *Abide With Me* were penned in the mid-19th century by an Anglican vicar, Henry Lyte, and are an exhortation to God to remain close by, even in times of trials. That simple idea of steadfast resolve still resonates and for those fans lucky enough to have heard the lines ring out on Cup Final day, *Abide With Me* provides a glorious soundtrack of anticipation. The verses traditionally sung are:

> *Abide with me; fast falls the eventide;*
> *The darkness deepens; Lord with me abide.*
> *When other helpers fail and comforts flee,*
> *Help of the helpless, O abide with me.*
> *Hold Thou Thy cross before my closing eyes;*
> *Shine through the gloom and point me to the skies.*
> *Heaven's morning breaks, and earth's vain shadows flee;*
> *In life, in death, O Lord, abide with me.*

THE DUCK WALK

Non-leaguers Aylesbury United enjoyed their best FA Cup run in 1994/95 in reaching the third round for the first time in their history. Wins over fellow semi-pro sides Newport and Kingstonian put Aylesbury through to enjoy the plum draw of Premiership outfit Queens Park Rangers at Loftus Road as their reward. While Aylesbury attracted plenty of headlines for their cup run, they created as many again for a unique celebration they developed along the way. After overcoming Newport 3-2 in the first round, the Aylesbury team got down on their knees and waddled across the pitch in celebration. Fittingly for a club nicknamed The Ducks, after the famous local Aylesbury breed, the "Duck Walk" celebration was hatched. By the time United took on QPR, neutrals were hoping for at least one Aylesbury goal to allow another airing of the now famous celebration. Rangers though had other ideas and powered to a 4-0 victory. Happily, the *Match of the Day* cameras were present to capture United's post-match farewell to their fans; players on their knees, with arms aloft in a carefully constructed waddle provided the perfect swansong!

WHO ATE ALL THE PIES?

It's undeniable that developments in sports science have led to great advances in footballers' fitness. For some time now, more rotund players have become rarer and rarer to spot; the modern footballer now combines athleticism, pace and power. Footballers, though, were not always quite so lithe. At the end of the 19th and start of the 20th centuries, double FA Cup-winning goalkeeper William "Fatty" Foulkes achieved both admiration for his skills, and notoriety for his size. Foulkes could certainly play; over 400 senior appearances, mostly for Sheffield United, a league championship medal and an England cap sat alongside his two cup winners' medals. However, it was not for his triumphs that Foulkes is best remembered – he was a giant of a man, almost head and shoulders above most of his contemporaries. Although reports do vary as to his exact size and weight, he was commonly agreed to be some inches above six-feet tall and, in his later days, well over 20 stone in weight. Team pictures of the time show Foulkes resembling a dad lining up for his son's junior team. While Foulkes' size made him stand out from a distance, it was his fiery temperament that was just as much of a talking point; he had a temper, and he wasn't afraid to use it. The 1902 FA Cup Final was going to form with First Division side Sheffield United leading Southern Leaguers Southampton 1-0 with just minutes remaining, when Foulkes conceded a controversial equaliser. The Sheffield stopper was convinced that scorer Wood was offside, tying up his boots, when the ball came to him. Having famously lost to non-league Tottenham in the previous year's final, United were incensed at the prospect of another upset. None of the Sheffield team were as furious as Foulkes, and he alone decided to confront the match official with his version of events. Unfortunately for referee Tom Kirkham, Foulkes was in such a hurry to find him and air his grievances, that he stopped only to take off his kit, and without a thought of dressing, promptly pursued the referee. With news of an angry, naked, 20-stone keeper chasing him, Kirkham sensibly hid in the first place he could find – a broom cupboard – while Foulkes was restrained from breaking down the door. Thankfully, there were no TV cameras to record this particular post-match reaction and after United won the replay, no doubt Foulkes' frame of mind improved, but he remained a man to tread around carefully.

A LITTLE HELP FROM MY FRIENDS

The FA Cup was the last major English competition to accept sponsorship; that it held out for the longest time was probably testament to its enduring tradition, but as times change, so do traditions. The four major sponsors so far have not insisted on a name change in the way the League Cup has seen its title change from one major company to another; hence we have previously enjoyed the Milk Cup and the Littlewoods Cup among others, and currently the Capital One Cup. Instead, the FA Cup has insisted on a more subtle line; so we have heard of the FA Cup sponsored by various major companies. The sponsors so far have been Littlewoods Pools (1994-98), AXA (1998-2002), E.ON (2006-11), and Budweiser (2011-14). There was no sponsor between AXA and E.ON.

THE SOCIAL NETWORK

The FA Cup took its first tentative steps into the world of social networking in 2011 when the competition's new sponsors, Budweiser, announced that an extra preliminary round tie between Ascot United and Wembley FC would be streamed live through their Facebook page. It was the first time in the competition's history that such an early round had been covered by live TV cameras and it attracted an audience of more than 20,000 online viewers. The Facebook experiment, or promotional stunt depending on your point of view, was repeated 12 months later. Once again Wembley FC featured, this time against Langford, also from the fifth level of non-league football. Interestingly, this year's Wembley FC squad was bolstered by the presence of a plethora of recently-retired top professionals, including Graeme Le Saux, Ray Parlour and Martin Keown. Curiously, the ex-Argentinian World Cup striker Claudio Caniggia was brought in to make his FA Cup debut. While the glut of ex-pros coinciding with online launches may have had more than a whiff of publicity about it, the emergence of more streamed games on Facebook pages of the future should not be ruled out. It is quite possible that audiences might have the chance to click on to the early rounds in much greater numbers in the near future and any promotion of the early rounds, online or otherwise, might just help audiences realise there is a lot more to the FA Cup than a glamorous day out at Wembley.

BUDWEISER ARE THE LATEST SPONSOR TO ADORN THE FAMOUS TROPHY'S RIBBONS

CAPTAIN MARVEL

In English football in the 1980s, few players came close to Bryan Robson in stature or influence; he was the inspirational leader and captain of Manchester United and England. While driving teams on from his central midfield role, Robson seemed to have everything a modern midfielder needed: he could pass, he could shoot, he could head and he could tackle. This rare combination of qualities marked out Robson as the outstanding midfielder of his generation and brought him many successes, particularly in the FA Cup. With Liverpool dominating the league throughout the decade, United had to settle for cup successes. Robson played in three FA Cup Finals for United, each as captain, and three times he strode up the 39 steps of the old Wembley to lift the famous trophy. In 1983 United met already-relegated Brighton in the final and almost fell victim to an almighty upset. Four goals were shared between the teams, before Brighton's Gordon Smith famously missed a glorious late chance to win the cup for the Seagulls. United were not so remiss in a replay which Robson dominated. Fully justifying his status as the most expensive player in Britain, he scored twice in a 4-0 victory. Shooting home from outside the area and then popping up on the goal-line to force home a second, Robson gave a master-class in attacking from deep. In 1985 it was Norman Whiteside who hit the headlines with a sumptuous curling shot past Everton's Neville Southall to win United a second FA Cup in three years. Weeks earlier in a fiercely-fought semi-final against Liverpool, Robson had once again showcased his attacking verve with the opening goal. A quick exchange of passes by the halfway line with Frank Stapleton saw Robson gallop through before firing into the top corner from over 20 yards; it was inspirational stuff. By the time Robson collected the cup for the third time in 1990, United's wait for the league title had stretched beyond 20 years and pundits were predicting that boss Alex Ferguson could be sacked. United though kept progressing in the cup and once again, with goals in the semi-final and final, Robson was instrumental in leading them on. An older Robson narrowly missed selection for another triumph in 1994 against Chelsea, though he was still able to score in the semi-final against Oldham. When he bowed out of Old Trafford weeks later, Robson left behind some glorious FA Cup memories; always fiercely competitive, with an eye for a pass and for a goal, he graced the competition.

HAVE WE MET BEFORE? 2

Liverpool's 2001 triumph over Arsenal was third time lucky for the Merseysiders against their great North London rivals.

1950 – Arsenal 2 Liverpool 0

Bolstered by captain Joe Mercer and England cricketer Dennis Compton, the Gunners were too strong for a Liverpool team looking for their first FA Cup. Future Liverpool manager Bob Paisley suffered heartache at Wembley, being dropped for the match despite being a regular in defence all season and having scored one of the semi-final goals against Everton. Paisley had declared himself fit to play after a knee injury, but was surprisingly overlooked.

1971 – Arsenal 2 Liverpool 1

Already champions, Arsenal went into the match looking to complete the first league and cup Double in their history. Moments into extra-time, after a close, goalless 90 minutes, Liverpool's Heighway raced down the left wing to fire in at the near post. The Anfield men's joy was short-lived though as Eddie Kelly scrambled an equaliser before Charlie George hit one of the most famous goals in Cup Final history; his shot taking off like a firework before landing inside Ray Clemence's right post to secure the Double. For a time, George's distinctive celebration of lying flat on his back inspired schoolboys to celebrate their goals in similar fashion, by lying prostrate on playgrounds.

2001 – Arsenal 1 Liverpool 2

In the first FA Cup Final played outside of England, in Cardiff's Millennium Stadium, the Gunners enjoyed the better of the match, and led 1-0 with less than ten minutes to go. Things could have been even better for the Gunners had clear-cut appeals for handball against Liverpool's Stephane Henchoz been given, but with time running out Arsenal looked good to complete a hat-trick of final wins against Liverpool. Incredibly, a late Michael Owen double took the cup from Arsenal's grasp. The victory secured the second leg of a cup treble for Gerard Houllier's men, with the League Cup and Uefa Cup also won that year.

A HELL OF A BEATING!

In the 140 years since the FA Cup was first contested, countless teams have suffered sizeable defeats. Many goalkeepers and defenders have been left red-faced after suffering defensive slip-ups, howlers or just the misfortune to run into a vastly superior opposition. In the FA Cup of course, losing by one has the same end result as losing by a bucketful and that is the charm of its simple knockout format; if you don't win, you're out for another year, it's win or bust. That said, the margin of some victories and defeats can only linger in the memory, losing by two or three is one thing, but...twenty-six?! On 15th October 1887 the highly-regarded Preston North End team hosted Hyde United in the first round of that season's competition. At the time, Preston were a strong team with serious intentions; three years earlier they had been kicked out of the 1884 FA Cup for admitting paying their players, something still frowned upon in the early days of organised competition. By contrast, Hyde were a humble outfit who would have been considered outsiders when they arrived at Deepdale. Reports at the time suggested that Hyde had managed to rile their more illustrious opponents by refusing to play the game in midweek. Allegedly this provoked Preston into playing their strongest team, which was bad news for Hyde. Had the tie been a boxing match, United would surely have thrown in the towel early in proceedings as they were hugely outclassed; trailing 12-0 at half-time they conceded a further 14 in the second period, to total a staggering 26-0 defeat. Ironically enough, despite conceding 26 goals, goalkeeper Charles Bunyan was commended on his performance and his disaster at Deepdale did not stop him going on to forge a career coaching in Belgium. Preston certainly did not lack confidence in their own abilities as months after hammering Hyde, when they contested the 1888 FA Cup Final against West Bromwich Albion, unbelievably they asked to be photographed with the cup before the game had even been played! The idea was to show off the cup while they were still wearing clean kit. West Brom were not impressed, and went on to score their only two chances of the final to record a sensational 2-1 upset. Some 125 years later, Preston's 26-goal victory remains the biggest winning margin in all FA Cup ties. In the modern era of better organised and fitter players, it could be a record that easily endures for another 125 years.

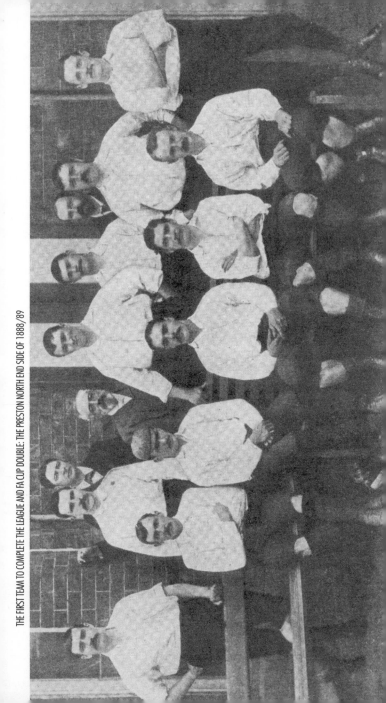

THE FIRST TEAM TO COMPLETE THE LEAGUE AND FA CUP DOUBLE: THE PRESTON NORTH END SIDE OF 1888/89

WELSH AIR AND A CORNER FLAG

In 1978, Northern Leaguers Blyth Spartans gave football fans across the country an FA Cup run to savour. They battled through four qualifying rounds to reach the first round proper before three successive 1-0 home victories saw them drawn away at Second Division Stoke City in round four. Spartans faced a strong Stoke team, boasting the emerging Garth Crooks and the experienced Howard Kendall. When Crooks nodded home to put Stoke 2-1 ahead, it looked as if, after eight rounds, Spartans' run was finally coming to an end. Two goals in the last couple of minutes though, including a net-buster from Terry Johnson, turned the tie around, and put Spartans into the last 16 of the cup. By the time high-flying Wrexham of the Third Division hosted Blyth in the fifth round, the nation had taken the men in green and white to their hearts and all eyes were fixed on the Racecourse Ground tie. Early on Johnson intercepted a poor back-pass to nudge Blyth ahead and they held that lead until the last minute of the match when controversy came calling. Chasing down the left wing, Wrexham's Shinton was challenged by Blyth skipper Waterson. Although the ball came off the Wrexham man last, referee Alan Hill erroneously awarded a corner. The first corner was headed back out for a second. As it was sent in, a gust of North Wales air toppled the corner flag and, on a point of order, the referee ordered a retake, even though the Blyth keeper had safely gathered the ball. When the third corner in a minute came over, for once Blyth failed to deal with the ball and Dixie McNeill barged it home to equalise for Wrexham. After being just seconds from the last eight of the cup, Blyth had to pick themselves up for a monumental replay, to be held in front of over 42,000 at Newcastle's St James' Park. After becoming the first non-league team since before the war to feature in the draw for the quarter-finals, a plum home draw against Arsenal was the prize for the winners. Sadly for Spartans they never quite recovered from conceding two early goals in the replay. By the time Johnson scored to halve the deficit there were less than ten minutes left, but on the night it was too little too late; Spartans' glorious march was finally stalled.

THE THINGS THEY SAY 2

"Newcastle were undressed! They were absolutely stripped naked!" BBC commentator David Coleman after Liverpool's final goal in their 3-0 win over Newcastle United in the 1974 final.

"Coventry are the favourites to win but the everlasting team-work of every bloomin' soul might, just might, pull it off." Schoolteacher and manager of non-league Sutton United, Barrie Williams, in his programme notes before they famously knocked out First Division side Coventry City in 1989.

"Manchester United in Brazil? I hope they all get bloody diarrhoea." Retired football manager Brian Clough reacting to Manchester United's decision to not enter the FA Cup in 2000.

"He has won the cup for Liverpool all by himself." ITV commentator Clive Tyldesley in the 2001 final, when a late Michael Owen double picked the cup out of Arsenal's pockets.

"It's nothing more than a consolation prize, an afterthought." Straight-talking Manchester United captain Roy Keane, in 2002.

"Making the FA Cup Final is a great lift for everyone: the manager, the staff, the fans, the players." The same straight-talking Manchester United captain Roy Keane, in 2004, prior to the final against Millwall.

"I just wanted to get good contact but the second one was just a dream goal. It was a dream goal and a dream day."

Steven Gerrard, a cup winner again, after scoring two spectacular goals in the 2006 FA Cup Final.

LEADING MEN

To manage and lead a team to victory in the oldest cup competition in the world is some achievement for any manager. To repeat or even better the feat puts any manager into an elite bracket most can only dream of. In the modern era, Sir Alex Ferguson heads the list with five Manchester United triumphs in the competition (1990, 1994, 1996, 1999 and 2004), closely followed by Arsenal's Arsene Wenger with four victories (1998, 2002, 2003 and 2005). Even those two greats of the modern game though have to bow to Aston Villa's George Ramsay, who led Villa to no less than six cup wins in 1887, 1895, 1897, 1905, 1913 and 1920. Ramsay was Villa secretary from 1884 to 1926, in the days when club secretaries were responsible for team affairs. His 42-year tenure saw a rich harvest for Villa, with six league championships accompanying the six cup wins. His longevity is unlikely to be challenged any time soon. Ferguson and Wenger would need to go into their 80s and 90s to catch him.

FAIR PLAY BY THE GUNNERS

When Arsenal entertained Sheffield United in the fifth round of the FA Cup in February 1999, a keenly contested last sixteen encounter was expected. First Division United may not have been fancied to win at the home of the defending Premiership and FA Cup winners, but after reaching the semi-finals a year earlier, the Blades were not going to be cannon fodder either. For most of the match typical cup-tie conventions were strictly adhered to; top flight giants Arsenal played with more guile and took an early lead; their second tier visitors battled hard and managed to level; and in classic cup-tie fashion, with just over ten minutes left the outcome was still in doubt. It was then that United striker Lee Morris needed treatment for a knock and it set in motion a chain of events, unprecedented in FA Cup history. The football rule-book was about to be turned upside down. When Blades keeper Alan Kelly deliberately kicked the ball high into the Highbury stands to allow Morris to be tended to by the physio, nearly 40,000 people at Highbury understood what was going on – players always kicked for touch to allow an injured player to receive medical attention. Unfortunately, when Ray Parlour threw the ball back to United, it became clear that not everyone quite knew what had been happening at the other end of the field. On his Arsenal debut, Nigerian striker Kanu was eager to impress, so when he saw the ball fall invitingly into space down the right wing he chased it and instinctively crossed for Marc Overmars to sweep home a winning goal. While the new signing thought he had just cleverly outwitted United's back-line, spectators, players and officials were aghast; an unwritten rule had just been trampled all over and the idea of fair play itself was hanging by a thread. When the final whistle signalled a controversial 2-1 win for Arsenal, trouble was brewing. Before United's legitimate complaints about unsporting behaviour and the honesty of the game could be aired, Arsenal acted decisively. With a speed of thought similar to Kanu's as he had dashed down the wing, Gunners boss Arsene Wenger immediately offered United a replay as the game had not been won in the right way. Quite what Kanu thought of his introduction to English football is unclear, though he did later explain he had simply not realised that anyone was injured and had quite unintentionally caused the storm. Wenger's and Arsenal's unique gesture was accepted straight away by United and was widely applauded in both the football and wider sporting world; even Fifa president Sepp Blatter commended the Gunners for upholding the traditions of fair play. The teams met for the second time ten days later and this time the match passed without incident as Arsenal once again won 2-1.

MARC OVERMARS'S CONTROVERSIAL GOAL IN 1999 THAT LED TO THE GUNNERS OFFERING TO REPLAY THEIR FIFTH ROUND FIXTURE WITH SHEFFIELD UNITED

NUMBER CRUNCHING 1

29.5 million: The number of viewers who tuned in for the tempestuous 1970 FA Cup Final replay between Chelsea and Leeds United. After a 2-2 draw at Wembley the teams met at Old Trafford in the first replay since 1912. Leeds were widely thought to have shaded the play over the two matches, but it was David Webb's late header that took the cup to Stamford Bridge for the first time. The matches are probably best remembered for their very robust style.

£1.8m: That is the prize money for this year's FA Cup winners.

114,815: The reported attendance for the 1901 final between Sheffield United and non-league Tottenham Hotspur, which was drawn 2-2. At the time, this was the largest ever crowd to attend a football match. A mere 20,000 made it to the replay at Bolton's Burnden Park, when Spurs memorably became the only non-league cup winners after a 3-1 win.

£30,250: The maximum amount of prize money a non-league team could win for reaching the first round proper this season – if they had started from the extra preliminary round.

2,000: The official attendance for the first ever FA Cup Final, played in 1872 at the Crystal Palace between Wanderers and Royal Engineers.

49: The number of goals scored by Harry Cursham of Notts County in the FA Cup in the 1870s and 1880s. Though Cursham's goal-scoring feats place him as the competition's all-time top scorer he never won the trophy. By the time County won their first and so far only FA Cup in 1894, Cursham no longer played for them.

1: The number of times a team has won the FA Cup after playing top-flight opposition in every round. Matt Busby's 1948 Manchester United side scored 20 goals as they beat First Division clubs in each round: Third round Aston Villa (A) 6-4; fourth round Liverpool (H) 3-0; fifth round Charlton (H) 2-0; quarter-final Preston North End (H) 4-1; semi-final Derby County (at Hillsborough) 3-1; final Blackpool (Wembley) 4-2.

WEMBLEY'S GREATEST UPSETS

FA Cup Final 1976: Manchester United 0 Southampton 1

Manchester United had been warned. Just three years before, in the most sensational Cup Final upset of them all, sixth-placed Second Division side Sunderland beat Leeds United, who had finished their season third in the First Division. Those same placings were repeated by United and Southampton in 1976, and so was the sensational outcome. Lawrie McMenemy's Southampton, like Sunderland before them, were rank outsiders to claim the first major trophy in their history. While Tommy Docherty's United boys were a vibrant, attack-minded team, they were only emerging; unlike Leeds, they had not spent season after season contesting the biggest prizes in football. In fact, United's youth and inexperience on the bigger stage probably did them no favours when things did not go their way. United started brightly enough and kept the Saints' keeper Ian Turner busy. He made smart saves from Coppell and Pearson and anticipated a Gordon Hill run expertly to block that chance too. For their part, Southampton's Mick Channon had a golden opportunity to open the scoring which United's stopper Alex Stepney saved with his left leg. In the second period McIlroy hit the underside of the crossbar with a header from a set-piece, but mostly Southampton seemed to be containing the Old Trafford men. With less than ten minutes left the Saints did get on the front foot for once, and Jim McCalliog lofted a clever ball in between United's defenders. Bobby Stokes reacted quickest and without a second's hesitation he hit the bouncing ball into the bottom left of Stepney's net. For United, a season of much admired, free-flowing football went unrewarded, while Southampton had their hands on the most glamorous domestic prize. After the final whistle Tommy Docherty vowed to take United back to Wembley to win the cup 12 months later and it was to be a promise he kept as United's attacking verve continued the flowing season. Another promise was kept when striker Bobby Stokes, in a sign of the very different times the match was played in, won a car for scoring the first goal of the final, only to reveal he could not drive! That did not matter to Stokes or his Southampton fans though who were sent into orbit by their afternoon at Wembley.

CUP FINAL FIRSTS

Winners – All those years ago in 1872, Wanderers beat Royal Engineers 1-0 with a Morton Betts goal, in front of 2,000 people. Little did they know what they had started!

Non-league finalists – Sheffield Wednesday, then known as The Wednesday, reached the 1890 Cup Final while still playing in the Football Alliance. The 20,000 crowd saw Blackburn romp home 6-1.

Non-league winners – Before they even joined the Football League, Tottenham were cup winners. Their 1901 team finished fifth in the Southern League, but managed to defeat First Division outfit Sheffield United 2-1 in a replay.

Double winners – In the first ever league season, 1888/89, Preston coupled winning the title without losing a game (a unique feat until Arsenal's Invincibles of 2003/04) with a 3-0 FA Cup triumph over Wolves to become the first winners of the Double.

Radio broadcast – The famous 1927 final, when Cardiff beat Arsenal to take the cup out of England, was the first to be broadcast live on the radio. The phrase "back to square one" referred to a grid of the pitch which the *Radio Times* had published to help listeners know which part of the field the ball was in.

TV broadcast – The 1938 final between Preston and Huddersfield was the first to be broadcast live on BBC television. The match was only decided when Preston were awarded a penalty in the last minute of extra time. The estimated audience was put at 10,000.

Got your number – The first FA Cup Final to feature players with numbered shirts was the 1933 match between Everton and Manchester City. Everton's white shirts displayed numbers 1–11, while City's blue shirts continued 12-22. It was Everton who were left counting the goals as they comfortably beat City 3-0, allowing their legendary number nine Dixie Dean to collect the cup.

Both ends – Charlton defender Bert Turner had an eventful afternoon at Wembley in the first post-war Cup Final in 1946. There were only five minutes left when Turner's left boot turned a shot from Derby's Dally Duncan into his own net to open the scoring. Within a minute though, Turner made amends by firing home an equalising free kick from more than 20 yards out; by doing so he became the first man to score for both sides in a Cup Final. Turner's efforts proved to be in vain for Charlton however, as Derby ran out 4-1 winners in extra time.

THE FIRST-EVER FA CUP FINAL PENALTY SHOOTOUT CLIMAXED WITH JENS LEHMANN SAVING PAUL SCHOLES'S PENALTY

Orange ball – When Sunderland upset all the odds to defeat Leeds in 1973, they did so with a unique match-ball. Conditions were so overcast before kick-off that the referee Ken Burns opted to use an orange ball, rather than white, for the match. In Cup Final history this has never happened before or since.

Sending-off – Manchester United's Kevin Moran was giving his marching orders in 1985 by policeman Peter Willis after upending Everton's Peter Reid.

Missed penalty – Liverpool's John Aldridge had slotted home 11 spot-kicks throughout the season, but kick number 12 was pushed away by Wimbledon's cup-winning captain, keeper Dave Beasant, in 1988's Wembley upset.

Penalty shoot-out – After 120 turgid, goalless minutes, Arsenal beat Manchester United 5-4 on penalties with Jens Lehmann saving from Paul Scholes in the 2005 final.

HEAT OF THE MOMENT

When the Victorian writer Rudyard Kipling penned some famous lines about "keeping your head when all about you are losing theirs" he had a point. The coolest of heads are required for big matches like an FA Cup Final; what no player wants is to be so overcome with a moment, an event or occasion that they faint. Unfortunately that is exactly what happened to Ipswich Town's 1978 hero, Roger Osborne. Going into the final, Ipswich were not fancied to do well; they had finished 18th and it seemed Arsenal, with the likes of Liam Brady and Malcolm Macdonald in their ranks, boasted more potential match-winners. The match turned out very differently to what was expected though as Ipswich produced some fast-flowing, attacking football that repeatedly cut Arsenal open – three times the men from Portman Road hit the woodwork through Mariner and Wark. Extra time seemed to be beckoning when with just 13 minutes left David Geddes sprinted past Sammy Nelson down the right flank and his cross was only half cleared by Willie Young. The ball fell perfectly for Roger Osborne's left foot and he drilled it home past an exposed Pat Jennings in the Arsenal goal to score the winner. Moments later, exhausted and ecstatic, Osborne fainted and was immediately substituted. His early exit did not ruin his day though as his goal turned out to be the only one of the match and it won the cup for Ipswich.

THE FIVE-MINUTE FINAL

Historically, Manchester United and Arsenal have dominated the FA Cup, yet when they met in the 1979 final neither team was dominating much; United had finished ninth under Dave Sexton while Arsenal were just ahead of them in seventh slot. With little between the teams, a close match was expected, with Arsenal marginal favourites due to their team boasting one of the outstanding talents of the time in the gifted Irishman, Liam Brady. A first half of few opportunities saw Arsenal take two that came their way. Midfielder Brian Talbot stabbed home a David Price pull-back from close range early on, before Frank Stapleton nodded home Brady's cross to double the Londoners' advantage before the break. United huffed and puffed in the second half but to no great effect and the final looked to be petering out to a straightforward Arsenal win. Even when United's Scottish man-mountain, Gordon McQueen, stuck out a long leg to steer the ball home with four minutes left, Arsenal seemed just a nervous glance or two away from seeing the game out. It was then that this most ordinary of finals took the most extraordinary of twists. Barely a minute later, chasing a Steve Coppell pass, Sammy McIlroy burst into the Arsenal defence and managed to tiptoe past O'Leary, Walford and Young before slowly rolling the ball under the advancing Pat Jennings. While United's players were ecstatic at their unbelievable comeback, Arsenal looked wiped out; they had both hands on the trophy and somehow let a winning lead slip from their grasp. As players, spectators and viewers at home all looked forward to 30 minutes of extra time, Brady picked the ball up in midfield. It would be stretching things to say Brady, exhausted as he was, ran at full speed, but he skilfully evaded a couple of challenges before finding his left-winger Rix. Most times, the wide-man's cross would have been collected without drama by United's keeper Gary Bailey, but this time the young stopper misjudged the flight, waving at the ball as it arced over him, on to the foot of the on-rushing Alan Sunderland. The man with the perm knew where the goal was, and simply prodded home behind Bailey's back to win the cup for Arsenal. The unforgettable last five minutes of the 1979 final ensured it became etched in the minds of everyone who saw it, proving once again you predict the Cup Final at your peril.

ICONIC GOALS – STEVEN GERRARD

The 2006 Cup Final pitched West Ham United and Liverpool together and the Londoners were clear underdogs. Although the newly-promoted Hammers had enjoyed a credible top-half finish under Alan Pardew, Liverpool had finished a strong third and, only 12 months before, had enjoyed a magnificent and miraculous Champions League final triumph. In archetypal FA Cup fashion however, things did not go according to plan. West Ham found themselves 2-0 up within half an hour, thanks to a Jamie Carragher own goal and a Dean Ashton rebound. Although Liverpool replied almost immediately through a smart Djibril Cisse volley, the half-time hiatus saw a shock on the cards. If the watching millions thought the frenetic first half would take some beating, they were wrong; more improbable twists and turns lay in store in a final of rare drama. Gerrard's arrowing volley drew the teams level, only for a much-debated Paul Konchesky cross-shot to nudge West Ham ahead once more. With the clock ticking down, it looked like Liverpool had finally used up their supply of footballing miracles and the cup would be going back to Upton Park for the first time in over a quarter of a century. The 90 minutes were up when Liverpool launched another desperate raid on the West Ham defence. When Danny Gabbidon headed a John Arne Riise cross over 30 yards away from his goal, it seemed certain that the claret and blue ribbons needed to be dusted down and wrapped around the famous trophy. With the ball bouncing away from the West Ham net, Liverpool's Steven Gerrard galloped towards it, and without breaking stride to survey the scene around him, hit the ball instinctively. The contact Gerrard made with the ball was perfect; technique, power and accuracy came together in a split second as Liverpool's captain drilled the ball into the bottom-right corner of Shaka Hislop's net. To score a goal like that on any stage would be memorable, but to score that most spectacular of equalisers, in the last minute of one of the most dramatic Cup Finals for decades was sublime. Melchester Rovers used to have a player called Roy Race who would score impossible goals each week, but he never played at Wembley, or Cardiff's Millennium Stadium – where the 2006 final was held – he only ever played in a comic strip. Gerrard though, turned the day into his own comic strip; lighting up the nation's pubs, clubs and living rooms with a one-man masterclass in making the impossible look easy.

STEVEN GERRARD FIRES HIS ICONIC CUP FINAL GOAL IN 2006 AGAINST WEST HAM

GREAT GOAL, SIR!

The author Barry Hines is better known for talking with his pen rather than his feet; but judging by his much-loved novel, *A Kestrel for a Knave*, he knows a thing or two about football as well. The book chronicles the tough teenage years of Billy Casper, growing up in a Yorkshire mining community and includes an iconic portrayal of the fifth round of the cup in a PE lesson. In the film version, *Kes*, rather than spend time worrying about the pace of his pupils' progress, Brian Glover's PE teacher, Sugden, worries about the pace of the players he handpicks for his own Manchester United team as they take on Tottenham Hotspur. United keeper Billy Casper soon lets in a soft goal and is instantly rewarded with an expertly-aimed heavy ball to the midriff from his furious teacher. Controversy quickly follows as, after blatantly diving, Sugden awards himself a penalty, which he gleefully converts at the second attempt. However, despite all his best efforts at fixing the outcome, the cup tie ends in misery for the teacher/player/manager/commentator/Bobby Charlton-style midfielder, as his United boys go on to concede a late winner. With "great goal, sir" still echoing in his ears, Sugden extracts more revenge on his unreliable keeper by blasting him with both boiling and freezing water in the showers. Glover's superb performance as the maniacal teacher may not have done much for that noble profession, but both book and film do nicely capture the fervour and frenzy of football fans facing a big cup tie – the big kid in us all!

THE FINAL COUNTDOWN

When Manchester City went to Wembley for the 1934 FA Cup Final against Portsmouth they were determined to make up for their 3-0 defeat to Everton 12 months earlier. After their loss in 1933, City captain Sam Cowan had toasted Everton with the hope that the next team to win the cup would be his own Manchester City. Cowan's words were to take on a prophetic ring. City lined up with a young goalkeeper, Frank Swift, in their ranks and within half an hour he was at fault for the opening goal. Playing without gloves on a wet surface, Swift dived to his right to collect a speculative 20-yard shot from the splendidly named Septimus Rutherford. The ball squirmed under the inexperienced keeper's dive and into the net, leaving City behind at half-time and Swift distraught in the dressing room. City striker

Fred Tilson tried to raise his young keeper's spirits by predicting that he would score twice in the second half, and, in a curious clairvoyant fashion, that is exactly what happened. Two Tilson goals in the last 20 minutes meant the cup was on its way to Maine Road for the second time. Despite the turnaround in City's favour, Swift found the end of the game difficult. A photographer behind his goal was counting down the minutes, and then seconds remaining, in full hearing of the keeper. Whether it was City's dramatic late comeback, the tension of being so close to claiming the cup, or the speaking-clock photographer, it all proved too much for Swift who promptly fainted at the final whistle. Happily, when he came around City were the new cup winners and the young man between the sticks certainly stuck around; playing nearly 400 games for Manchester City and 19 times for England. Tragically, Swift died in the Munich air disaster.

FA CUP TROPHIES

The present FA Cup trophy, which will be presented this May, is actually the fourth incarnation of the famous old cup. In the same way that Dr Who occasionally regenerates into a newer, fresher model, once or twice the trophy itself has needed replacing. The original FA Cup was used from 1872, but it came to an infamous end when it was stolen from a Birmingham bootmaker in 1895. That first cup was nicknamed the "little tin idol" and its replacement fared little better, lasting only until 1910 when it became so fragile it needed replacing. The new version was made in Bradford and soon ended up back there, as, for the one and only time in their history, Bradford City reached and won the final in 1911. For just over a century, the most recognisable trophy in English sport has stayed looking the same, although wear and tear meant the 1911 version had to be replaced by an exact replica in 1992. Of course, like us all, the cup takes its share of bumps and bruises each year and needs some restorative work. The present trophy is taken to a silversmith in London every year for repairs before it is handed out to the next victorious captain. Any dents or imperfections are ironed out as the cup is heated, reshaped and silver plated once again, making it ready for its big day at Wembley. Engravers will then add on the name of each year's winners to the bottom of the trophy, to further add to the history of the most famous cup in football.

DID YOU KNOW?

Second tier finalists: In 140 years of competition, there have been just 13 finalists to come from the second tier of English football and lose on the big occasion. They are Bolton Wanderers (1904), Barnsley (1910), Huddersfield Town (1920), Wolverhampton Wanderers (1921), West Ham United (1923), Sheffield United (1936), Burnley (1947), Leicester City (1949), Preston North End (1964), Fulham (1975), Sunderland (1992), Millwall (2004), and Cardiff City (2008).

Second tier winners: In the first 100 years of FA Cup competition, only four teams from the second tier managed to win the FA Cup. In the following eight years though, underdogs enjoyed a purple patch, as three second tier teams triumphed. However no second tier club has won the FA Cup since West Ham did so by beating Arsenal 1-0 in 1980. The other second tier winners are Notts County (1894), Wolverhampton Wanderers (1908), Barnsley (1912), West Bromwich Albion (1931), Sunderland (1973), and Southampton (1976).

Hat-tricks of final wins: Only two teams have ever managed to win the FA Cup in three successive seasons. They are Wanderers, who did it in 1876, 1877 and 1878, and Blackburn Rovers, whose hat-trick came in 1884, 1885 and 1886.

ICONIC GOALS – RICKY VILLA 1981

Tottenham Hotspur needed a replay to win the FA Cup in 1981, finally beating Manchester City 3-2. Though it had featured the rarity of one man, Tommy Hutchison, scoring for two teams, the first game was more drab than dramatic as Spurs and City played out a 1-1 stalemate. Tottenham's Ricky Villa was famously substituted in the original match as his influence had waned, but he was to take on a starring role in the replay. Less then ten minutes had been played when Villa's fortunes changed; he cleverly followed up a Steve Archibald shot to put Spurs ahead. Three minutes later though City equalised with a sublime Steve MacKenzie volley into the top corner from the arc of the penalty area. With both sides having rediscovered their attacking edge, the game was already a cracker. City took a second half lead from Reeves's penalty, only for Spurs to level through Crooks's finish. Going into the final ten minutes it was hard to pick a winner; like championship boxers going the full distance, both teams knew how to hurt each other, yet had given everything and were exhausted. Sometimes a mistake from a tired player helps to settle a big occasion, or

FA CUP WINNER RICKY VILLA RECREATES HIS FAMOUS WEMBLEY WINNING GOAL AGAINST MANCHESTER CITY IN 1981

someone manages to find a knockout blow from somewhere. On this occasion, it was the latter and the man who delivered it was Ricky Villa. The disconsolate substitute on Saturday had already redeemed himself with his early strike and industrious performance, but with eight minutes left Villa wrote himself into FA Cup folklore with a dazzling winning goal. When he received a square pass from Galvin, Villa was still 30 yards from goal and there seemed to be no imminent danger. With tiredness creeping in though, City defenders Ranson and Caton allowed Villa to run directly at them on the edge of the penalty area. He built up some momentum and when both defenders went to challenge him together, he dribbled past. Villa first went outside on his right foot, then inside on his left, before switching back again to his right to slam the ball past the advancing Joe Corrigan. In just seconds Villa had toyed with and then destroyed City's defence; Ranson and Caton suddenly looked like they had swopped their boots for ice skates, as they stumbled and staggered around, almost drunkenly, after Villa. Fittingly, that goal was the winner and Ricky Villa, the man with the ball glued to his feet, made football look easy.

THE SKY'S THE LIMIT

When Arsenal and Huddersfield fans made their way to Wembley for the 1930 FA Cup Final, they were all treading a familiar path. Both sides had made recent losing visits to the new national stadium and were keen to make amends. An added interest lay in Arsenal manager Herbert Chapman meeting up with his old team Huddersfield. As a matter of mutual respect for him, the two teams went out side-by-side for the first time at a Cup Final. After the Wembley spectators settled down to enjoy the match, Arsenal's Alex James took just 16 minutes to open the scoring. His terrific shot from the edge of the penalty area put the Gunners on their way to a first FA Cup triumph. Before either team could add any further goals though, the 90,000-plus spectators had good reason to take their eyes off an absorbing encounter; slowly, above the stadium, appeared the unlikely outline of the world's largest airship – the German airship, the Graf Zeppelin, was calling. News reports of the time talk of a sinister zeppelin hovering over Wembley, but how much hovering it did as opposed to how much flying by at a steady rate of knots is open to debate. What is for certain is that the crew of the 776-foot long airship, almost foreshadowing Sky TV coverage of later years, had the best view in the house. As Huddersfield tried and failed to rein in Arsenal, the

Gunners added a late second to secure the first of what has since become many FA Cup victories. However, it is the image of the German airship floating over Wembley's open ends, rather than the shots of captain Tom Parker holding the cup aloft, that have endured from the 1930 final – a peacetime image of a portentous time.

TOP DRAWER DIDIER

Ivorian striker Didier Drogba seemed to take quite a shine to the FA Cup. Four times during his stay in England, Drogba was part of FA Cup-winning Chelsea teams and he became the first man to ever score in four separate finals. Drogba was an impressive forward; combining power and pace with some delicate skills. In the first Cup Final played at the rebuilt Wembley in 2007, Drogba scored the late extra-time winner, deftly finishing off a smart one-two with Frank Lampard to defeat Manchester United. Two years later it was Lampard's turn to score the winning goal against Everton after Drogba had earlier risen high to power an unstoppable headed equaliser. When Chelsea retained the trophy in 2010 they beat already-relegated Portsmouth courtesy of a solitary Drogba strike. This time the striker showed off another part of his repertoire by side-footing a curling free kick home from over 20 yards. In the 2012 victory over Liverpool, Drogba scored another deciding goal with a low angled left-footed shot for his fourth goal in four FA Cup Finals. The unique collection of strikes from Drogba showed not just that he was a player for the big occasion, but he was a player with a bit of everything. He scored goals with his head, with either foot and with power and precision; most definitely a big man, for a big occasion.

HORSES FOR COURSES

When Chelsea and Leeds United squared up to each other for the 1970 Cup Final, the match was not only a clash of two of the top three teams in the league that season, but it was also a final which guaranteed a new name on the old trophy. With a great occasion on the way and a much anticipated match to look forward to, the eyes of the nation turned to Wembley. However, all was not well at the national stadium; millions of television viewers, 100,000 spectators and the two sets of players and officials were not greeted with the lush, green Wembley turf, but instead saw a pudding of a pitch. Even before a ball was kicked, the playing surface resembled a farmer's ploughed field and with good reason; that year's Horse of the Year show had only finished a week before. Ironically enough, that year's leading show jumper was a pony called Stroller, yet few of the players were able to stroll around the furrowed Wembley surface. At one point in the second-half, with Leeds pressing to regain their advantage, ITV commentator Brian Moore remarked how the "ball wouldn't bounce", and, unbelievably, it wouldn't. As it happened the quagmire did little to quash the excitement as Leeds twice led, only to be pegged back both times by Chelsea, who went on to win a fiercely contested replay at Old Trafford – on a pitch that hadn't hosted any horses.

DID YOU KNOW?

Hat-trick heroes: In the 131 FA Cup Finals played so far, only three men have ever scored hat-tricks. William Townley got the first, for Blackburn Rovers in their 6-1 win over The Wednesday in 1890; and James Logan scored the second as Notts County beat Bolton Wanderers 4-1 in 1894. The last came in 1953 as Stan Mortensen netted three times in the famous "Matthews Final" which saw Blackpool beat Bolton 4-3.

Lord Kinnaird: The giant of the early years of football was so well thought of by his peers that when the FA Cup trophy needed replacing in 1911, the obsolete trophy was given to Kinnaird, a five-time winner himself, to keep. It remained in his family until 2005, when it was bought at auction by current West Ham chairman David Gold for £478,000.

Player-managers: In the modern era, there have been three examples of player-managers taking teams to the FA Cup Final. Kenny Dalglish was still an important player for the Reds in the Double-winning Liverpool team of 1986, playing half of the league games and most FA Cup ties. Dalglish played the whole 90 minutes at Wembley as Liverpool beat their great rivals Everton 3-1. Eight years later Chelsea reached the final against Manchester United under Glenn Hoddle's stewardship. By then, Hoddle's magnificent playing career was winding down and he felt the full force of a rampant United, playing the last 20 minutes in a 4-0 reverse. Dennis Wise similarly came up against a strong Manchester United when he led second tier side Millwall to the 2004 final. Wise and his team lived up to their billing of rank outsiders and never troubled United in a comprehensive 3-0 defeat. Wise played almost the entire match, a full 16 years after his first FA Cup Final appearance, in Wimbledon's famous victory over Liverpool in 1988.

KENNY DALGLISH WAS THE FIRST PLAYER-MANAGER TO LEAD A TEAM IN THE FA CUP FINAL

THE MAGIC OF THE CUP

There are not many things that all football fans agree upon, but the idea of the underdog upsetting the formbook and knocking out more fancied opposition has endured. Over the years many non-league outfits have toppled league opponents and teams like Yeovil Town (in their non-league days), Altrincham and Telford United have been regular scourges of Football League sides, to the great delight of neutrals everywhere. The business of amateurs making monkeys of the professionals started in the 1880s when, in their inaugural league season, Stoke City achieved an unwanted first. Non-league Warwick County travelled to Stoke's Victoria Ground in the first qualifying round on 6th October 1888, to take on the league newcomers. In an early example of a team choosing to concentrate on their league campaign at the expense of progress in the cups, Stoke played their reserves against Warwick. Whether this was related to a 7-0 defeat the first team suffered at Preston, just days before, is unclear, but the decision backfired badly. County beat Stoke 2-1 in what is now recognised as the first proper cup upset. Weeks later, County won their next qualifying round tie against Aston Shakespeare, but their dreams of reaching the first round proper ended with a 5-1 defeat against Burton Wanderers, who would become a Football League club six years later. Warwick County went the opposite way; after being founder members of the Midlands League in 1890, they were expelled the following season for not fulfilling their fixtures. Warwick had however left their mark, and showed that sometimes, part-timers could just topple their professional rivals – the magic had started.

THE RIBBONS

The annual adornment of the FA Cup trophy itself with the winning team's ribbons seems to have gone on forever, and it certainly has lasted a lifetime. The first recorded instance of it however goes back to one of the most famous finals of all – the solitary triumph of a non-league team, when Tottenham Hotspur, then of the Southern League, won the cup way back in 1901. In the first match of the final, Tottenham drew 2-2 with highly fancied Sheffield United in front of the first ever recorded football crowd of more than 100,000. The replay at Bolton Wanderers' Burnden Park saw Spurs go on to sensationally win 3-1, and when they received the trophy their own colours of navy and white were attached to the cup, courtesy of the wife of one of the Spurs directors. The idea of the winning colours being astride the trophy immediately became an established part of Cup Final celebrations, and, over a century on, it seems like the winning ribbons are here to stay.

ONE MAN AND HIS HORSE

When Wembley was built in 1923, it had an official capacity of 127,000 making it the biggest stadium in England by a distance. The new Empire Stadium was considered to be big enough to house crowds for any occasion – England internationals or FA Cup Finals. Just days after Wembley was completed it was put to the test in the 1923 FA Cup Final between Second Division side West Ham and middling top-division Bolton Wanderers. The three previous finals had been played at Chelsea's Stamford Bridge to less than capacity crowds and that, coupled with the size of the new stadium, helped the FA to assume there would be room for everyone; they were wrong. Unbelievably to a modern audience, the authorities did not think to make the game an all-ticket affair. This resulted in many, many thousands going up to Wembley on the day, hoping to see both the match and the new stadium. As the crowds arrived, the giant Wembley bowl filled to overflowing, and yet spectators kept on coming; some waited patiently in queues, some hopped over the walls to guarantee their entry. Estimates of the numbers who were in the stadium vary from 200,000 to 300,000, and while that can never be verified, it was commonly agreed that the official attendance of 126,047 was a massive underestimate and that the number of people inside the stadium and its vicinity was dangerous. With the overcrowding getting worse, the police resources were nowhere near enough to control the spectators. It was then that one officer, PC George Scorey, and his white horse, Billy, wrote their names into Wembley folklore without even kicking a ball. They walked up and down the pitch, marshalling the crowds effectively; whether it was through skill, or luck, or a testament to conduct in the 1920s, PC Scorey and Billy somehow kept the crowds in order and prevented a disaster. Remarkably the game went ahead after only a 45-minute delay, with the well-ordered crowds fringing the four sides of the pitch, as close to the action as a referee's assistant. Police officers even had to clear spectators to allow corners to be taken, but the match was played and passed off successfully with Bolton winning 2-0. PC Scorey was publicly praised for his heroics and the FA went on to send him tickets – after they discovered how useful tickets could be – for later finals. That gesture was wasted on PC Scorey though as he never attended another match in his life.

THIRD TIER TEARS 1

No team from the third tier of English football has yet reached an FA Cup Final, though there have been some heroic runs to the last four. Here are just three, with more to follow later on.

1976 – Southampton 2 Crystal Palace 0

Malcolm Allison was known for many things in football, and one of them, his trademark fedora hat, first emerged on a thrilling cup run his Crystal Palace team enjoyed in the spring of 1976. With an eye for a gimmick, Allison's hat fitted the bill, but that year his Palace side did the talking for him on the pitch too with some notable victories against higher opposition. First Division Leeds United, Second Division Chelsea and then Sunderland all fell to the recently rebranded Eagles. Although Allison's Palace were decisively beaten by Southampton in the semi-final, he had succeeded in putting them back on the football map, with better days just around the corner.

1984 – Watford 1 Plymouth 0

Plymouth earned their semi-final spot after winning 1-0 away at First Division side West Bromwich Albion, and then repeating the trick at Second Division Derby County. Argyle enjoyed a rare day in the national spotlight when they played Graham Taylor's Watford at a sunny Villa Park, but it was Taylor's effective team who secured their Wembley berth courtesy of a smart header from George Reilly.

1997 – Middlesbrough 3 Chesterfield 3
Replay – Middlesbrough 3 Chesterfield 0

En route to the last four, Chesterfield knocked out a soon-to-be-relegated Nottingham Forest of the Premiership and followed that up with a quarter-final victory over fellow third-tier outfit Wrexham. Sadly, there was heartbreak for the Spireites in the last four at Old Trafford when a controversial refereeing decision denied them a 3-0 lead against top flight Middlesbrough, who fought back to level at 2-2, and then win the replay.

LAZARUS RIDES AGAIN

At the turn of the millennium, Tranmere Rovers got themselves into a very handy habit of being drawn against, and then knocking out

THE GOAL THAT NEVER WAS FOR CHESTERFIELD AGAINST MIDDLESBROUGH IN THE 1997 FA CUP SEMI-FINAL

top flight teams in major cup competitions; in just under a year and a half, Rovers knocked out seven Premiership sides. Arguably, the most memorable of the lot was a February night at Prenton Park in 2001, against Glenn Hoddle's Southampton. Hassan Kachloul, Jo Tessem and Dean Richards all netted for the Saints in the first half to surely put the tie out of Rovers' reach at 3-0 down. It was as though Southampton were extracting revenge on Tranmere for the six recent Premiership scalps the men from the Wirral had claimed; the underdogs were receiving a bowlful of come-uppance and there seemed no way back. Few of the Tranmere fans could have imagined it at half-time, but one of the FA Cup's most startling comebacks was about to swing into action. When Tranmere manager John Aldridge introduced ex-Everton striker Stuart Barlow for the second period to add some pace and goal threat it was probably more in hope than expectation, yet things soon began to change. Within 15 minutes of the restart, Rovers' veteran striker (and scorer of Everton's winner in the 1995 Cup Final) Paul Rideout skilfully steered an Andy Parkinson drive home and when he then nodded home a second from a Jason Koumas corner with 20 minutes left, the Prenton Park faithful started to believe in miracles. With ten minutes to go, Rideout climbed between two static defenders to nod home his third of the night and bring Rovers level as the Premiership side wobbled. Solid, mid-table Southampton were there for the taking, and just minutes later, after a little head-tennis in the Saints penalty area, Stuart Barlow took the chance he was given to fire Rovers ahead. Home fans on the Bebington Kop were ecstatic, as, unbelievably, another cup shock was unfolding. What brought about the startling reversal is difficult to pin down. Complacency from Southampton might have come into it; substitute Barlow certainly played a part; it was the old gunslinger himself though, Paul Rideout, who changed things around the most. Tranmere had a miracle match, but with a steer and a nod in the right direction, it was Rideout who played the Lazarus role to perfection.

I.O.U.

Back in 1990, after three trophyless years, there was much speculation that Alex Ferguson could be about to lose his job at Old Trafford. Struggling in the league, United were under pressure when they travelled to Nottingham Forest for their third round tie in January 1990. Fans were unhappy, newspapers were grumbling and the vultures seemed to be out for Ferguson. United laboured through the first half, but when they were in need of inspiration, two of their strikers combined to provide it. Mark Hughes bent a through ball around the Forest defence and rookie striker Mark Robins smartly ran on to head home the only goal of the game into Steve Sutton's net. That set United on a run that would culminate in a Wembley win against Crystal Palace and it launched the start of the most successful period in their history. Robins went on to become a well-respected striker; he was combative and had an eye for goal at several clubs, but he might still be best remembered by many for that winner at the City Ground. The idea that Ferguson really did face the sack had United faltered at Forest was always denied by chairman Martin Edwards. Sir Alex though, as he went on to become, undoubtedly owed a large debt to a more than handy little striker from Oldham.

THE DISAPPEARING CUP

For the third time in eight years, Midlands rivals Aston Villa and West Bromwich Albion met in the FA Cup Final of 1895. With one win each to their names, Villa forged ahead in their local rivalry by winning the final with a solitary goal (reports describe a goalmouth scramble which finished with either John Devey or Bob Chatt scoring) to take the cup back to Birmingham once more. Villa's pride at their second triumph was enormous and they were happy to parade the trophy to their fans back at home. Months later, in September, the cup was still being shown off and it was scheduled to spend a night in the shop window of a local bootmaker, William Shillcock. When he opened up the following morning however, the most famous cup in football was missing as burglars had broken in and stolen it. To Shillcock's and Villa's horror, the trophy was never recovered. Over 60 years later, an 83-year-old called Harry Burge came forward to solve the mystery of what had happened to the trophy. In a newspaper interview, Burge declared that he himself had stolen the cup to melt it down for fake coins. Whether that account was reliable or not, the 1895 trophy never returned and the FA had to commission a replica based on miniature versions Wolves had received two years earlier.

LORD OF THE MANOR

When professional football was only just emerging as a sport, one man stood out as a major influence on how the game developed. With his red beard and long trousers, the distinctive figure of Arthur Kinnaird was a hard man to miss. A bit like a latter-day Seb Coe, he combined his own sporting excellence with a major administrative role in the sport that he had graced. First though came Kinnaird's extraordinary playing career and he could certainly play a bit. Of the first 12 FA Cup Finals that took place, Kinnaird played in a staggering nine of them, winning three times with Wanderers and then twice more with Old Etonians. His game was versatile and at different times he played in all positions, including goalkeeper. Similar to a modern-day Roy Keane, Kinnaird's style attracted a certain renown in his own playing days, with one commentator from the *Athletic News* claiming he particularly enjoyed "manly, robust football", euphemisms no doubt! While keeping goal for Wanderers against Oxford University in the 1877 final Kinnaird mistakenly carried the ball over his goal-line to score the first prominent own goal in football history. Though Wanderers went on to win the match after extra time, Kinnaird, a man of much influence, complained so vehemently about the award of the first goal against him that for decades it was expunged from the records and the official result was given as a 2-0 win. That took some explaining, as Wanderers' first goal came with only minutes of the original 90 left, which of course would have meant extra time should never have been played. If there was confusion about the 1877 final, there was no mistaking Kinnaird's joy after winning the cup for the fifth time in 1882 with Old Etonians. After being presented with the cup, Kinnaird eschewed the raising-of-the-trophy-above-his-head celebration, and instead, to everyone's surprise, he promptly stood on his head in front of the stand! Kinnaird's influence on the early days of football was impressive in his own playing days, and it was scarcely less so after he hung up his boots. He served as the president of the FA for over 30 years and oversaw a period of monumental change in the way football was played and followed. Football went from being a park game played by amateurs, to being an organised, professional game played in front of thousands; it would become first the national game, and then the global game.

ARTHUR KINNAIRD PLAYED IN NINE OF THE FIRST TWELVE FA CUP FINALS

NUMBER CRUNCHING 2

484 million: The estimated global television audience for the 2005 FA Cup Final between Arsenal and Manchester United. The fixture underpins the worldwide appeal of the oldest domestic cup competition in the world, with well over 100 countries across the globe continuing to broadcast the showpiece match.

126,047: The official crowd figure given for the inaugural Wembley FA Cup Final played in 1923. Bolton and West Ham contested a match which became more famous for its enormous crowd, who were surrounding the pitch, rather than any events actually on the pitch.

1872: The first ever FA Cup competition, won by Wanderers after a 1-0 victory over Royal Engineers. That year, just 15 teams entered the competition.

1938: The first fully televised FA Cup Final, with Preston beating Huddersfield 1-0 in the last minute of extra time.

1927: The first FA Cup Final to be broadcast live on BBC radio. Cardiff's 1-0 win over Arsenal was the only time, so far, that the cup has gone out of England.

758: How many teams will compete in this season's FA Cup competition. While in theory any side could battle their way through to the final, the teams involved at the start of the competition are a very long way from the Wembley arch. The FA Cup starts with the extra preliminary round, then there is a preliminary round, before the four qualifying rounds take place. League 1 and League 2 teams join the competition in the first round proper, Championship and Premier League from round three, then the numbers are reduced further and further until there are only the semi-finals and final left to play.

SEEING IS BELIEVING

It is sometimes said that a picture can tell a thousand words and a quick look at this image from a pivotal moment in the 1954 FA Cup Final seems to prove the point. With almost an hour gone, West Bromwich Albion were trailing 2-1 to Preston North End and their hopes of a fourth cup triumph were receding. It was then that Preston right-half

Tommy Docherty blatantly bundled over Albion's Ray Barlow in the penalty area, leaving striker Ronnie Allen to convert the spot-kick. At the moment Allen took his kick, West Brom keeper Jimmy Sanders was unable to watch from some 100 yards away and he turned his back. A mixture of nerves, worry and fear meant the Albion keeper could not bear to watch as Ronnie Allen drew Albion level. The tension of the moment might have got to Sanders just then, but he held his nerve for the remainder of the game, conceding no further goals and hopefully getting to see Frank Griffin's late winner for West Brom.

SO NEAR AND YET SO FAR 1

In 2008, Havant & Waterlooville, of Conference South, reached the fourth round of the FA Cup for the first time. When the Hampshire part-timers were then paired with Liverpool, the 19 times league champions, five times European champions and seven times FA Cup winners, the romance of the cup was put firmly back on football reporters' agendas. With five leagues and over 120 league places separating the two teams, there was little talk of the Hawks of Havant swooping for the kill; instead, it seemed sure to be a tale of lambs to the slaughter. Whether Liverpool's players let the huge gap in pedigree affect them is unclear, but as the game went on it was clear that something was very amiss in the middle of the Reds' defence. From a left-wing corner, truancy officer Richard Pacquette found himself unattended in the six-yard box and powered home a header in front of the Kop to put Havant ahead. Although Liverpool levelled through a fine Lucas effort, the drama had further acts to run. With Havant pressing down both flanks Liverpool's defence needed to maintain their vigilance. What they did not need was for two defenders to crash into each other to allow Havant's Alfie Potter into the penalty area with the Liverpool goal in his sights. Potter's strike took a mighty deflection off Martin Skrtel, but none of the 6,000 Havant fans were bemoaning that, as for the second time the ball nestled into the Liverpool net. The surreal-looking scoreboard, registering Liverpool 1 Havant & Waterlooville 2, did not stay that way for long. By the interval the teams were level again and Liverpool went on to put three more past Havant to eventually run out 5-2 winners. Rafa Benitez's boys were not exactly showered with praise for their performance and instead all the plaudits went south to the non-leaguers who, for a brief period, had threatened the most seismic of cup shocks.

THIRD TIER TEARS 2

No team from the third tier of English football has yet reached an FA Cup Final, though there have been some heroic runs to the last four. Here are two more, with another instalment to follow later on.

1955 – Newcastle United 1 York City 1
Replay – Newcastle United 2 York City 0

The highlight of York's run was their fifth round tie against First Division side Tottenham Hotspur. Although the game was played on a slippery, snowy, muddy pitch which would barely have been declared fit for a ploughing competition, the conditions did not stop York splitting Spurs open repeatedly, coming from behind to claim a famous 3-1 win. After beating Notts County of the Second Division in the quarter-final, York then took on the might of First Division Newcastle United. City were held to a 1-1 draw in the torrential rain in the first semi-final at Hillsborough, but York's Wembley hopes then disappeared in front of a packed Roker Park, losing to an early and a late goal.

1959 – Luton Town 1 Norwich City 1
Replay – Luton Town 1 Norwich City 0

The highlight of Norwich City's progress to the last four was a startling 3-0 toppling of Manchester United's Busby Babes in round three. That match signalled what Norwich were capable of, and, spearheaded by centre forward Terry Bly, they carried on their excellent form knocking out higher league opponents in Cardiff City, Sheffield United and most memorably Tottenham Hotspur. The Canaries could not quite repeat the trick in a replayed semi-final, losing out narrowly to Luton Town of the First Division, but the heroics of that 1959 team are fondly remembered. So much so, in fact, that a song, *The Ballad of Crossan and Bly*, was penned in their honour decades later.

THE GOOD, THE BAD AND THE UGLY

Despite several later highlights for him, the spring of 1991 was a time when Paul Gascoigne might just have been at the peak of his very considerable powers. Still glowing in the post-Italia 90 euphoria, Gascoigne was now universally known: he was Gazza the cheeky chappie; he was Gazza the boy who had cried in Turin; he was also Gazza the footballer, who left opponents for dead, as he fired

GAZZA CELEBRATES SPURS' FA CUP SEMI-FINAL WIN OVER ARSENAL IN 1991

Spurs to the FA Cup Final. The expensively assembled Tottenham Hotspur team were never close to winning the championship but had once again saved their best form for the FA Cup, with Gascoigne their catalyst. By the time Spurs and Arsenal lined up for the first Wembley semi-final, Gascoigne had already contributed five goals to the campaign including some memorable, mazy runs, of the type that Lionel Messi has since trademarked. Returning from injury it took Gascoigne only minutes to leave an indelible mark on the old Wembley stadium. Fully 35 yards from David Seaman's goal, the number eight decided to test out his England colleague. Like in the comic strips when Roy Race used to belt goals in for Melchester Rovers from every angle, Gascoigne simply thumped the ball in to the top-left corner of the net. The power behind the shot looked like it could have taken off Seaman's hand or broken the net; it was Gascoigne at his audacious best. In the post-match interview, Gascoigne's excitement was clear for everyone to see; his high spirits were not hard to fathom. Weeks later Tottenham returned to Wembley to face a Nottingham Forest side desperate to give Brian Clough a first FA Cup win. Like all players approaching an FA Cup Final, Gascoigne's anticipation had been steadily rising, but by kick-off his mood had turned to agitation; on a day requiring cool heads, Gascoigne was about to lose his. Within minutes of the start once again Gascoigne had the crowd gasping, this time however it was an ugly, chest-high challenge on Forest's Garry Parker that drew sharp intakes of breath. Referee Roger Milford decided that the assault on Parker did not merit a caution, so Gascoigne's frenzy was left unchecked. Only 15 minutes into the match Gascoigne was at it again, recklessly and dangerously felling Forest full-back Gary Charles, this time thigh-high. While Charles recovered to play on, Gascoigne was in trouble; he stood in the Spurs wall to defend Stuart Pearce's missile of a free kick, which opened the scoring, but his knee was ruptured and his career looked to be in ruins. In time Gascoigne did recover and played many more times at the highest level, his career though took a different path after the Cup Final. Further injuries and off-the-pitch issues meant the player of 1991 was seldom seen in future and Gascoigne, more than most players, went on to experience the full range of what football could throw at someone; the good, the bad and sometimes the ugly.

THERE'S ONLY ONE TIM BUZAGLO!

Although Second Division side West Bromwich Albion were not enjoying a good league season in 1990/91, when they were paired with Woking of the Isthmian League in the third round of the cup, the Baggies would have expected to make progress. With the match to be played at The Hawthorns and opponents Woking in the second tier of non-league football, West Brom might have been forgiven for expecting a straightforward afternoon. After 45 minutes, although Woking had given a good account of themselves, they trailed to Colin West's header and nothing remarkable seemed to be in the air. It was in the second period that computer operator and Gibraltar international cricketer Tim Buzaglo took centre stage. The pacy forward with an eye for goal hared past West Brom's ponderous centre-backs to first level, and then to put Woking ahead. A superb sweeping move split West Brom open like a slice of cake and Buzaglo put the icing on the top with a firm left-footed finish for his hat-trick. Woking's fourth was added before Albion's consolation second was greeted with boos from the home fans. Incredibly for West Brom their season would only get worse; manager Brian Talbot was sacked within days and new man Bobby Gould could not arrest the slide to a first ever relegation to the third tier. By contrast, Buzaglo's goals catapulted him into the spotlight; that evening he was whisked away to the *Match of the Day* studios to enjoy Des Lynam's quips about there being only "one Tim Buzaglo", and to hold the match-ball for the nation to see. Buzaglo and Woking went on to enjoy a fourth round tie at Everton's Goodison Park in front of more than 30,000 fans. Everton's top flight know-how was too much for the minnows, but only just, as Woking bowed out 1-0.

MOST GOALS SCORED IN AN FA CUP TIE

Ted McDougall – 9, Bournemouth 11 Margate 0 1971/72

Harold Atkinson – 6, Tranmere 8 Ashington 1 1952/53

George Best – 6, Northampton Town 2 Manchester United 8 1969/70

Ted McDougall – 6, Bournemouth 8 Oxford City 1 1970/71

Duane Darby – 6, Hull City 8 Whitby Town 4 1996/97

Denis Law – 6, Luton Town 2 Manchester City 6* 1960/61

*match abandoned, Luton won the replay 3-1

SUPER MAC

Ted MacDougall achieved the unique feat of scoring nine goals in a single cup tie for Bournemouth in 1971. If McDougall had never played in the first round tie against non-league Margate in November 1971, he would still have been remembered as a good, maybe very good, striker after more than a decade of league football brought him over 250 league goals. However, it was his startling performance in scoring nine out of the 11 goals Bournemouth put past Margate keeper Chic Brodie that became his signature piece. MacDougall notched five in the first half and came close to doubling that tally with four more in the second period as Bournemouth tore Margate apart in the rain. The striker earned himself a unique place in the competition's history as no player before or since had ever scored more than six goals in an FA Cup tie. Ironically enough, MacDougall himself had equalled that old record of six in a cup tie the year before when Bournemouth blitzed Oxford City 8-1. Scoring goals by the bucket-load catapulted MacDougall to national prominence; within a week he was taking calls to appear for a Rest of the World team in Geoff Hurst's testimonial and within a year he had signed for Manchester United. Although moves to Old Trafford and later West Ham were not successful, MacDougall went on to score plenty more for Norwich and Southampton, leaving little doubt that the man from Inverness was more than a nine-goal wonder.

THE BURNDEN PARK DISASTER

On 9th March 1946, English football suffered a terrible tragedy when 33 fans were crushed to death, and 400 more were injured, at an FA Cup quarter-final tie between Bolton Wanderers and Stoke City. The dreadful events of the day had a terrible simplicity about them; the crowd wanting to attend the game was far in excess of what the stadium could comfortably hold – too many people were in too small a space to be safe. Even today, the popularity of football in 1946 is hard to imagine. Professional football had been absent from people's lives for seven long, war-torn years, and the enthusiasm with which its return was greeted was enormous. Regular league games were selling out all over the country, never mind FA Cup quarter-finals. An added excitement for many fans queuing up to watch Bolton and Stoke that day was the presence of Stanley Matthews in the Stoke side; it was a big cup tie, with a big star and an inevitable big crowd. When the stadium gates were shut 20 minutes before kick-off, Burnden Park was

ALAN PARDEW CELEBRATES HIS WINNING GOAL AGAINST LIVERPOOL IN THE 1990 FA CUP SEMI-FINAL

already dangerously full. Estimates of the number of fans in the ground range from the officially quoted 65,000 to upwards of 80,000. Whatever the actual numbers were, there were far too many. The sheer pressure of the waiting thousands outside resulted in gates being broken down and when a wall inside the ground collapsed a consequent crush ensued. For a time, the seriousness of the situation was not realised as the match kicked off. Within 20 minutes though, the dead and injured were being taken away as the scale of the disaster was beginning to become apparent. Rightly or wrongly, the game was completed amid fears of disturbances. The events at Burnden Park led to a reappraisal of football stadium safety and the inquiry into the disaster called for smaller stadium capacities and for greater vigilance to be paid to the number of spectators allowed entry. Of course, the issues of spectator safety and how best to accommodate large crowds would not go away. A little over four decades later, in another cup tie, this time at Hillsborough, the same issues would once again resurface in tragic circumstances. Lessons about how to properly, and safely, look after fans, it seemed, were just not learnt.

HOME AND AWAY

For the only time in its long history, the FA Cup was played as a two-legged competition in 1945/46. With the nation beginning to slowly emerge from the Second World War, regular league football was not yet at the pre-war levels so the simple idea of expanding the competition was hit upon. Apart from the semi-finals and final, all rounds were to be played both home and away. The first three rounds were held on consecutive Saturdays, while the later rounds were played on Saturdays and Wednesday afternoons, as stadiums had no floodlights in those days. In the austere climate of post-war Britain, with resources rationed and lives waiting to be rebuilt, sport, and particularly football, was a very welcome diversion for millions. As the nation's appetite for normality in all walks of life returned, crowds were huge, with several gates topping 70,000. While football's post-war boom was about to take off, there were practical drawbacks with having two-legged ties. On a sporting note, in many cases, a decisive first leg result rendered the second leg redundant, while there was always the possibility that the eventual winners may have lost several matches on their way to securing the trophy. On an economic note, the huge attendances, particularly on Wednesday afternoons, were a major headache for employers who could find themselves minus many employees. As the proper league re-emerged for 1946/47, the FA Cup reverted back to its original, one match, knockout format so Derby's two-legged triumphs remain an anomaly in the competition's history.

JEEPERS KEEPERS 1

For three successive years in the 1950s without meaning to, goalkeepers played starring roles in FA Cup Finals. Bert Trautmann, Ray Wood and Harry Gregg all had reasons to remember, and to forget, their Wembley appearances. In 1956, Manchester City's Trautmann reached Wembley looking to make up for the disappointment of 12 months previously when his City team had lost to Newcastle. Trautmann was more than an outstanding keeper; he was an outstanding character too, with a unique background. He had fought for the Germans on the Russian Front, been a prisoner of war in England for three years and then worked in a bomb disposal unit, before finally being spotted by City while playing for St Helens Town. While Trautmann began to establish himself at City, he inadvertently took on a role even more demanding than keeping goal for one of the biggest clubs in the country. As a German man, less than ten years after the end of the Second World War, Trautmann achieved more for Anglo-German relations than any raft of government initiatives might have managed. By being an autograph-signing, friendly and talented goalkeeper, Trautmann greatly helped to demolish the caricature of nasty Germans. With a background like his, Trautmann was probably tougher than most, and at Wembley in 1956 he certainly showed it. City were leading Birmingham 3-1 with just 16 minutes to play when Trautmann dived courageously at the feet of the onrushing Peter Murphy. The keeper won the ball on the edge of his six-yard box, only to suffer a dreadful impact to his neck which knocked him out. When he came around, Trautmann assured his trainer he was fine to carry on (this was long before the days of substitutes), but spent most of the remainder of the match clutching his very sore neck. In that closing period Trautmann continued to defend his goal with an iron resolution, at one point even managing to rush off his line to thwart another Birmingham attack before recoiling in agony. The dreadful pain though, which caused him to hold the side of his neck, was not going to stop Trautmann from playing his part in a cup-winning team; he was determined not to let his team-mates down and he didn't, with City running out 3-1 winners. Days after City won the cup, Trautmann was diagnosed as having a broken neck and he faced months of rehabilitation before later going back to reclaim his role as City's number one. However, it was that awful injury and the way Trautmann refused to be defeated by it, which came to define him as a man without peers in the bravery stakes.

THIRD TIER TEARS 3

No team from the third tier of English football has yet reached an FA Cup Final, though there have been some heroic runs to the last four. Here are more, with Wycombe Wanderers' 2001 run to the last four covered in more depth later on.

1937 – Sunderland 2 Millwall 1

In 1937, Millwall became the first third tier team to reach an FA Cup semi-final and they did it in spectacular style, with wins against some of the best teams in the country. Convincing early victories over Aldershot and Gateshead were followed by London derby wins against Fulham and First Division Chelsea before the Lions despatched title-chasing Derby at home. A packed Den then saw Millwall take on and beat another championship hopeful when mighty Manchester City came to town. City were enjoying a long unbeaten run and with stars like Frank Swift and Peter Doherty they were clear favourites but it was Millwall's day, with two goals from Dave Mangnall proving the difference. The Wembley dream stayed alive when Mangnall opened the scoring in the semi-final against reigning league champions Sunderland, but there was a sting in the tail for the Lions as their opponents came from behind to win 2-1.

1954 – Port Vale 1 West Bromwich Albion 2

The year Port Vale reached the FA Cup semi-finals was probably their best ever. They won the Third Division North by nine points, conceded a record low of 21 goals and lost only three times in the league. An emphasis on strong defence paid dividends in their cup run too, as top flight Cardiff City and cup-holders Blackpool were both despatched 2-0. For the Blackpool game, heavy rain had made the Vale Park pitch desperately muddy, which did not suit Stanley Matthews' men, and when Albert Leake scored twice in the first half the tie was beyond Blackpool. After winning 1-0 at Orient in the sixth round, Vale took on one of the top teams in the country in West Brom. Vale scored first, again through Leake, but this time they could not hold on and Albion's winner came from a controversial penalty award.

DAVE BEASANT BECAME THE FIRST GOALKEEPER TO SAVE A CUP FINAL PENALTY AND THE FIRST KEEPER TO LIFT THE CUP AS CAPTAIN

DROPPED FROM A GREAT HEIGHT

When Manchester United reached the 1990 FA Cup Final against Crystal Palace they were a very different proposition to today's club; an inconsistent, mid-table team, they had talented players, but they had not then accrued a winning habit. Alex Ferguson was only just beginning to shape a team in his image and the Wembley showpiece gave him, and United, a chance to show that they were ready to become winners. One of Ferguson's many strengths, both then and now, is his fantastic drive and determination; he simply does not tolerate failure. Never was this better illustrated than in that 1990 final, when Ferguson had reason to doubt his number one goalkeeper, Jim Leighton. After a thrilling first match, United were fortunate to finish with a 3-3 draw and a replay. Although for the watching fans, with its twists and turns, the game had been a feast to gorge upon, Ferguson saw things differently. Leighton twice went for crosses, twice ended up in no-man's land, and twice conceded avoidable goals during a torturous afternoon. That Ferguson and Leighton went back a long way, and had shared many trophies together for Aberdeen, counted for nothing. With a replay he had to win coming up fast Ferguson acted ruthlessly, dropping Leighton and opting to play back-up choice Les Sealey instead. The decision proved to be as successful as it was shocking; Sealey played a blinder in the replay and kept a clean sheet as United won the cup 1-0. Leighton played only one more League Cup tie in United colours before ignominiously slipping out of Old Trafford.

THE UPS AND THE DOWNS

As FA Cup runs progress, players and managers often mention the beneficial effects of getting closer to Wembley. The general idea is that the winning habit takes root and good cup form can then be translated into good league form too. Although this must often be the case, there have been some notable exceptions.

1925/26 Bolton Wanderers 1 Manchester City (relegated) 0

For the first time ever, one of the cup finalists was relegated. City's fate was confirmed after the Cup Final when they lost their last league fixture 3-2 at Newcastle, when even a draw would have kept them up.

1968/69 Manchester City 1 Leicester City (relegated) 0

Leicester's miserable season went from bad to worse as two weeks after they lost their third Cup Final of the decade they were also relegated. A fixture pile-up meant the Foxes had to play five more games after their Wembley defeat, with everything hinging on a last match against Manchester United which ended in a 3-2 reversal.

1982/83 Manchester United 2 Brighton & HA (relegated) 2
Replay Manchester United 4 Brighton & HA 0

When Brighton's chartered helicopter flew the team towards Wembley the Seagulls' league fate had long been decided. They finished the season eight points adrift of safety after only nine league wins, saving their best performances for the cup. Had a late chance in extra time been converted Brighton would probably have become the first team to combine a unique double of relegation and FA Cup triumph.

1996/97 Chelsea 2 Middlesbrough (relegated) 0

Just six days before the Cup Final, a final-day draw at Leeds had placed Middlesbrough in the bottom three confirming their relegation. The Teessiders though were furious at an earlier decision in the season to deduct three points from their league tally after they had postponed an away fixture at Blackburn, citing player illnesses. The football authorities dismissed Boro's claims, and the three-point penalty later became crucial as Boro were relegated by just two points.

2009/10 Chelsea 1 Portsmouth (relegated) 0

By the time Portsmouth reached their second Cup Final in three years things were starting to go seriously wrong at Fratton Park. In just one season the club experienced several different owners, acute financial problems and also entered administration. Portsmouth were deducted nine points as the penalty for going into administration and became the first team to be relegated that year.

HOME FROM HOME 1

The Cup Final at Wembley is now a long-standing tradition, but the competition enjoyed many different homes in the early years.

1872 Kennington Oval – A major cricket ground for well over a century, but eight years before WG Grace starred there in the first Test match in England, the Oval hosted the first FA Cup Final. Wanderers' 1-0 win against The Royal Engineers set the ball rolling in the world's oldest domestic cup competition.

1873 Lillie Bridge – The London venue saw Wanderers retain the cup after beating Oxford University. The low 3,000 crowd was in part due to the match being played in the morning to avoid clashing with the varsity boat race.

1874-1892 Kennington Oval – In the years the Oval hosted finals, increasing attendances – from 2,000 in 1872 to 25,000 in 1892 – reflected public enthusiasm for the competition.

1886 replay The Racecourse, Derby – The first final outside London saw Blackburn Rovers complete a hat-trick of wins on Derby County Cricket Club's home patch.

1893 Fallowfield, Manchester – Wolves beat Everton 1-0 to secure their first cup victory. The 45,000 crowd was too large for the small stadium and overcrowding was an issue on the day. The stadium survived until near the end of the 20th century, but now the site holds student accommodation.

1894 Goodison Park – Nearly 40,000 watched Notts County's Jimmy Logan score a hat-trick in the Magpies' 4-1 win over Bolton. At the time, Goodison was just two years old and was the country's first purpose-built football stadium.

1895-1914 Crystal Palace – A vast arena large enough to hold three crowds in excess of 100,000, and, but for the First World War, might have held many more finals. The site is now home to the well-regarded athletics stadium of the same name.

1901 replay Burnden Park – Bolton's old ground held one final as Tottenham Hotspur beat Sheffield United 3-1, the only time a non-league team has won the cup.

1910 replay Goodison Park – When Everton hosted their second cup final, and first replay, over 60,000 packed in to watch Newcastle beat Barnsley.

1911 replay Old Trafford – Bradford City won their only FA Cup so far. They lifted a new trophy, the replica of which is still used today.

1912 replay Bramall Lane – Barnsley also won their only FA Cup after a replay. The only goal in two matches came two minutes from the end of extra time against West Brom.

THE ROYAL BRASS BAND AT THE 2010 WEMBLEY FA CUP FINAL

SUPER SUNDAY

These days the Super Sunday billing for English football has become a routine part of Sky TV's football presentation, when any number of live matches are on offer to the armchair audience. Before Sky Sports was around though, the BBC pioneered the idea of a live double-header for the nation to watch. They screened the FA Cup semi-finals of 1990 and it was an inspired choice. Champions-elect Liverpool lined up against mid-table Crystal Palace at Villa Park in the first tie. Liverpool could not have been hotter favourites; earlier in the season they had severely clipped the Eagles' wings in a 9-0 league win at Anfield and it seemed inconceivable that Palace could reverse their fortunes. The game started off according to the script with Liverpool holding possession and taking a lead into the interval, but after the break some funny things started to happen. Whether it was Gary Gillespie's injury or not, Liverpool began to defend like strangers, and soon found themselves trailing 2-1. With less than ten minutes to go further twists came; first, Steve McMahon levelled matters and when Liverpool converted a penalty moments later, it seemed an upset was no longer on the cards. Incredibly though, Andy Gray equalised and with the Liverpool defence in pieces Palace still managed to hit the bar in normal time. Extra time brought no respite for Liverpool and when Alan Pardew nodded home from another uncleared cross, it was Palace who were off to their first FA Cup Final; worthy winners, their 9-0 humbling a distant memory. If that had been a treat for TV viewers, a little later that afternoon a second helping of cup drama was served up to the nation by Manchester United and Second Division Oldham Athletic. The Latics were in sparkling form in the cups that year; they had already reached Wembley in the League Cup Final and the United team they faced were far from invincible – manager Alex Ferguson had not yet won a single trophy in his tenure. Oldham's attacking intent was soon rewarded when they scored first, but United gave as good as they got and equalised, before twice leading, only for the Latics to twice equalise. Six goals were shared at Maine Road before United narrowly won the replay 2-1. Viewers watching the drama unfold in their living rooms had gorged themselves on an unprecedented feast of FA Cup football and with it, the idea of televised semi-finals took root. The days of simultaneous Saturday semi-finals would never be returned to.

THE GIANT-KILLERS – SUTTON UNITED 1989

When Coventry City arrived at the picturesque Gander Green Lane to play non-league Sutton United in the third round of the 1989 FA Cup, the footballing world was a very different place. The Premiership did not exist, City had won the cup just 18 months before and, incredible to think of it now, the Sky Blues were fourth in the top flight, while Sutton occupied 13th spot in the Vauxhall Conference. On paper, it looked a straightforward tie, but Sutton had read a different script. Managed and marshalled by English literature teacher Barrie Williams, Sutton went on to write some footballing chapters of their own with an inspired display. Williams' men scrapped ferociously, belying the 101 league places between the two teams and edged what looked like being a goalless first half. Minutes before the break though, City were undone by a near-post corner which was flicked on to the head of defender Tony Rains who powered home the most significant goal in his 600-plus games for United. Seven minutes after the restart David Phillips ran through the Sutton back-line before smartly converting and restoring parity. Unfortunately for City, things were not on an even keel for long; just six minutes later the Sky Blues were again found wanting at defending a set-piece. A cleverly pulled-back corner and cross gave wide-man Matthew Hanlon a volley he, and the 8,000 fans present, will never forget. In the final half-hour City woke up and chased the game. England international Cyrille Regis was an inch away from equalising, while Wembley hero Keith Houchen hit the bar; the Sky Blues even rattled both bar and post within seconds, but Sutton held on. When the curtain came down on Coventry's calamitous afternoon, few who were present could dispute Sutton were worthy winners. The story goes that Sutton had spent part of the morning practising their set-pieces, only for manager Williams to cut short the session as his charges got everything wrong. The part-timers though, raised their game for the afternoon's bigger stage and it was Williams' set-piece routines that sent Coventry crashing. Williams enjoyed some fleeting fame of his own as he dipped into his store of great literature to provide the press with some notable quotes. None were more appropriate than the ones he ran in the programme notes for Coventry's visit, using Rudyard Kipling to exhort his team to greater efforts:

> *It ain't the individual*
> *Nor the Army as a whole*
> *It's the everlasting team work*
> *Of every bloomin' soul.*

UNITED WE FALL

In February 1971, Don Revie's Leeds United were flying; their season promised much as they were top of the First Division, in the Fairs Cup quarter-finals and facing a seemingly routine FA Cup fifth round tie at Fourth Division Colchester United. By contrast, Colchester were flirting with the top half of their division but had struggled to put a consistent run of results together for most of the season. In pools-speak, it looked an away banker. Prior to the match, there were no clues that anything untoward might be on the horizon, Colchester had hit no great heights and Leeds no great lows; the idea of an upset seemed barely credible. Yet after 45 minutes, some very untypical, calamitous defending from Leeds left them 2-0 down. A poorly defended free kick allowed Ray Crawford to head home and the same veteran striker then cleverly scored while on the floor after colliding with Paul Reaney. After the interval, a long bouncing ball into the Leeds area resulted in another dreadful mix-up between Reaney and Sprake, which allowed Dave Simmons to head Colchester into a fairytale 3-0 lead. The scoreline was simply not believable. Although Leeds did rally and scored through Norman Hunter and Johnny Giles, an equalising goal would just not come. Colchester keeper Graham Smith joined in the heroics minutes from time when in mid-air he brilliantly caught a close-range ricochet that had BBC commentator David Coleman declaring: "It must be one of the saves of the season." It was that kind of day for Colchester; everything stuck. The result signalled a difficult time for Leeds; they lost the league by a point to Arsenal and though they took the Fairs Cup from Juventus, their season was viewed as one that could have been better. Colchester could not repeat their performance in the next round, losing 5-0 at Everton, but after causing the shock of that, and many other seasons, they revelled in their moment of FA Cup magic.

SPRING IN HIS STEP

For well over 100 years the FA Cup has had a fantastic ability to generate excitement, emotions and passion in equal measure; there are some days when players, management and supporters just can not help reacting to the unfolding dramas in front of them. The Cup Final of 1966 between Everton and Sheffield Wednesday was such a day. If you wanted a template for a final of fluctuating fortunes this

TWO-GOAL HERO MICHAEL OWEN CELEBRATES DURING LIVERPOOL'S 2-1 WIN OVER ARSENAL IN THE FIRST MILLENNIUM STADIUM FA CUP FINAL IN 2001

match would take some beating. Everton trailed to a well-hit Jim McCalliog goal at half-time, before Wednesday's David Ford scored a close-range second to double the Owls' advantage. With almost an hour gone, Wednesday looked to have a firm grip on the FA Cup and despairing Everton looked like they had a mountain to climb. But just seven sensational minutes later the pendulum swung completely as surprise Toffees selection Mike Trebilcock brought Everton level with two thumping strikes. For any fans, watching your team play in a Cup Final, watching them clearly losing then watching them stage a speedy and unlikely recovery, would provoke an outpouring of joy. That is exactly what happened to one particular Evertonian, Eddie Kavanagh, who was about to achieve a fame almost parallel with his Goodison heroes. When Trebilcock equalised, Kavanagh needed to show his delight; shouting and screaming, cheering and cavorting were not enough for Kavanagh; he simply could not contain his joy, it had to come out. With sheer ecstasy coursing through his veins, Kavanagh started probably the best-natured pitch invasion of all time when he raced towards Wembley's lush green turf. Once he got there, he simply kept going; across the length of the pitch, past the teams and towards Gordon West's goal at the far end of the stadium. Kavanagh's joy was boundless but unhappily for him, and memorably for the watching spectators, he was not alone for long; the errant Evertonian soon had police officers for company. Kavanagh outpaced the first chasing and flailing officer, who ended up flat on his face, but the second member of the constabulary was a different proposition. Seconds later, Kavanagh was superbly rugby-tackled by the second police officer and was left prostrate at the arc of the Everton penalty area. With braces showing and arms outstretched in a flat-on-your-back celebration, Kavanagh was now at the mercy of the law and soon found himself taken away by four officers. Although we will never know what Kavanagh might have done had he seen Everton's Derek Temple score the winner ten minutes later, he left a mark on the 1966 final almost as indelible as that of his Everton heroes. While spectators on the pitch are rightly frowned upon these days, for a high-spirited, spontaneous celebration, the 50-yard dash and good humour of Eddie Kavanagh leaves most celebrations trailing some way behind.

TROUBLED TIMES

The 1985 sixth-round tie between Luton and Millwall should have been another archetypal FA Cup match; high-flying Millwall of the Third Division had their eyes on a major scalp, that of struggling top-tier Luton Town. With a cherished semi-final place on offer, TV executives selected the game to be screened live, never imagining what they would soon be transmitting. The match, which Luton won 1-0, became an afterthought as Kenilworth Road witnessed scenes of dreadful crowd disorder, on a scale seldom seen in Britain, and certainly never before seen on live TV. Millwall fans simply rioted; they ripped up seats, invaded the pitch and fought battles with police. Whether in the comfort of your living room, or, worse still, present at the stadium, the events were appalling to watch and showed football in a dreadful light. Years later, it's hard to overstate how far following football in the 1980s was removed from the fashionable, polished, leisure pursuit it has since become; three decades ago football stadia could be harsh, unwelcoming, and, if your luck was out, threatening too. The riot at Luton should have been a massive wake-up for the football authorities, even a clarion call, that things needed to change; the days of decrepit stadia and poor spectator behaviour had to be consigned to the history books. Perhaps predictably though the riot did not encourage calm reflection or informed leadership, instead, a raft of instant solutions to the pernicious problem of spectator violence were heard. The Prime Minister, Margaret Thatcher, wanted ID cards; Luton's chairman, David Evans, wanted, and got, away fans banned; Chelsea chairman Ken Bates wanted fans behind electrified fences! Sadly, the Kenilworth Road disorder became another footnote in an ever-lengthening litany of football hooliganism; only when disaster struck on an unimaginable scale at Hillsborough four years later, were the deep-rooted problems of English football fully addressed.

SO NEAR AND YET SO FAR 2

FA Cup semi-finals are meant to be exciting, dramatic occasions; a bit like a great book or a film, they should grip you from start to finish with an unfolding, unpredictable narrative. If you mix in a comeback or two, a few goals and a massive talking point you have the recipe for the perfect semi-final, which is exactly what Chesterfield and Middlesbrough served up in 1997. It was top tier Middlesbrough of the Premiership v third tier

Chesterfield of the Second Division, and the gulf between the two teams was enormous. This expensive Middlesbrough vintage was a puzzle though; they had tremendous players in Fabrizio Ravanelli, Juninho and even Emerson, yet they spent the season fighting, and ultimately losing a relegation battle. With stories of Boro striker Ravanelli picking up a then staggering £40,000 a week, they were a financial powerhouse. Chesterfield, on the other hand, were from the other side of the footballing tracks, a classic collection of lower league players, some on their way up, some on their way down. If it was David v Goliath there could be no mistaking who was who; mighty Boro were Goliath, lowly Chesterfield were more like David's weedy little brother; they were surely just the warm-up act for the final. Delightfully, as the tie unfolded, nothing went as anyone had been predicting. Boro were reduced to ten men in the first half after Vladimir Kinder's sending off and Chesterfield took full advantage of their extra man. Andy Morris prodded Chesterfield ahead, and skipper Sean Dyche converted a clear penalty to put the third tier men 2-0 up. The watching millions began to prepare for history to be made; it seemed the Spireites were on their way to becoming the first ever third tier team to reach an FA Cup Final. When Ravanelli converted a low cross to make the score 2-1 the tie was in the balance again and it was then that Lady Luck took centre stage. Chesterfield continued to attack and their courage looked to be rewarded when Jonathan Howard seemed to smartly convert a chance from eight yards. The ball flew in off the crossbar before bouncing back over the line, but even without replays, it looked like it might be a goal; even the linesman flagged for it. Referee David Elleray, famously an Eton schoolteacher, ruled the ball had not crossed the line; sadly, he was wrong, the goal should have stood. If Boro rode their luck with the 'goal' that never was, they soon made the most of it by levelling through a Craig Hignett penalty before going 3-2 ahead in extra time when Gianluca Festa fired home a rebound. Though Chesterfield did secure a 3-3 draw with a late Jamie Hewitt header the feeling was that the Spireites had been wronged, and the wait for a third tier finalist goes on as Boro eased through the replay 3-0.

FA CUP FINAL 1987

In 1987, Tottenham Hotspur looked like they were on the verge of something special; they lined up as a who's who of English football: England star Glenn Hoddle, World Cup winner Ossie Ardiles, 48-goal

COVENTRY CITY'S 1987 FA CUP FINAL HERO KEITH HOUCHEN SHOWS OFF THE TROPHY AT WEMBLEY

striker Clive Allen and dazzling wide-man Chris Waddle were all stellar names who had enjoyed an excellent season. Coventry City, by contrast, were a ragbag of a team; their first-teamers were mostly gleaned from the lower leagues and they were usually too busy fighting relegation to be in the shake-up for any trophies. City were a workmanlike team, organised and gritty, but there was not much to suggest their 104-year wait for a major trophy was about to end. The final took no time to get going as inside ten minutes both teams had scored. In the first minute, Allen's near-post opener was his 49th of the season, but an unfazed Coventry were brought level when Dave Bennett nimbly rounded keeper Ray Clemence to score with a rare left-footed effort. That blistering start set the tone for a match that neither team could dominate; instead, it ebbed and flowed throughout; the pre-match predictions of Tottenham dominance were certainly wide of the mark. A defensive mix-up led to Gary Mabbutt's goal shortly before half-time yet although City went in trailing 2-1, doom and gloom were nowhere to be seen. In the first 45 minutes Bennett and Micky Gynn had provided midfield thrust, while also in the middle, Lloyd McGrath was quietly giving a masterclass in how to nullify a star player, as he shackled Hoddle from start to finish. There was room for optimism. Just after the hour mark, for the umpteenth time, Cyrille Regis rose high to flick a ball on. Keith Houchen picked it up, fed it to Bennett on the wing and smartly turned back towards goal. Bennett hit the perfect cross, arcing the ball around the full back, but away from Clemence, allowing Houchen a fraction of a second to gamble on a diving header. Houchen arrived like an airliner coming in to land, steering the ball home expertly; his gamble was rewarded with one of most spectacular goals to grace any Wembley final and at 2-2 the match was becoming a classic. City's winner, in extra time, was nothing like Houchen's graceful goal. Midfield action-man McGrath, improbably, found himself on the right wing and dashed down the line before crossing to whoever might be in the middle. Before Nick Pickering could try to get near to it, McGrath's cross struck Mabbutt's knee, and in that split-second the die was cast; the ball looped up high, dropped over Clemence and nestled in the far corner of the Tottenham net. For the first time City were in front, and that was how it stayed. The Sky Blues had finally won a major trophy, they had deserved to do so and had played a full part in one of the best FA Cup Finals ever seen. The Promised Land indeed.

THE RED DEVIL

The 1985 FA Cup Final between Everton and Manchester United was eagerly anticipated; United played attractive, attacking football under Ron Atkinson and Everton were the league champions who, just days before in Rotterdam, had won the European Cup Winners' Cup. Although Cup Finals do not always deliver the excitement we hope for, it was hard to see how this one could fail as two of the country's leading teams and many of the star players of the day were on show. Excitement though was not high on the list of adjectives for the millions watching, as both teams cancelled each other out. The contest was interesting, maybe even absorbing, but lacking in drama, until 12 minutes from time. United wide-man Jesper Olsen had possession on the right and, under pressure, cut infield to play a ball back to Paul McGrath. Not many people ever took the ball off McGrath, he was a supreme defender, but on this occasion Peter Reid had anticipated where the ball was going and he intercepted McGrath's first-time pass. Kevin Moran, McGrath's central defensive partner, was well positioned to cover and challenge the advancing Reid. Moran knew where to go and what to do; unfortunately, he was just a fraction of a second late. Reid was simply scythed down and sent tumbling across the turf. Although it was a clear foul, Moran had not gone in recklessly, or with malice, his timing had been out though and the referee had a decision to make. Peter Willis, a police officer by profession, saw Moran's challenge in clear terms; had Reid burst through successfully he would have had a clear goalscoring opportunity, the foul had prevented that happening and could only be punished by a dismissal. Moran acquired the notorious tag of being the first player to be sent off in almost 60 years of Wembley finals. Moran remonstrated with the referee and was aggrieved to be sent off the field, feeling an injustice had been done. For days afterwards he was then at the centre of a media storm debating whether he should be given a medal or not. The medal Moran did eventually receive turned out to be a winner's one after United went on to win the game in extra time, courtesy of a majestic curling shot from Norman Whiteside. Moran's dismissal probably made as many headlines the next day as the goalscorer Whiteside did, but it hardly mattered to United fans who once again were dancing around Wembley with the cup.

SOS ESSANDOH

When third tier Wycombe Wanderers enjoyed a marvellous run to the cup quarter-finals in 2001 manager Lawrie Sanchez could have been forgiven for thinking that Lady Luck was on his side. Wanderers had never been so far in the competition before and after beating three Division One sides, the prospect of playing Premiership outfit Leicester City was fantastic. Lower league clubs often have notoriously thin resources and Wycombe were no exception. They found themselves in the middle of an injury crisis shortly before their big tie at Filbert Street, having no-one fit who could play up front. Wanderers took the unprecedented measure of issuing an appeal for any available strikers who were not cup-tied to contact the club. When the story was run on the BBC's teletext service, Ceefax, it was spotted by a football agent who had an unemployed player in Finland on his books; someone called Roy Essandoh. Without having scouted him, Wycombe immediately offered Essandoh a week-to-week contract. After appearing as a substitute before the cup tie, Essandoh found himself on the bench again for the quarter-final. With the game level at 1-1, manager Sanchez decided to take a gamble on the man who had not been able to find a club in Finland. On the sidelines tensions rose with the Wycombe boss being sent off for berating an official, but on the pitch it was Essandoh who rose higher than everyone else to nod home a sensational late winner. Wycombe were in their first ever FA Cup semi-final thanks to a winning combination of Roy Essandoh and Ceefax. Wycombe went on to narrowly lose their semi-final to Liverpool and Essandoh was released at the end of the season after almost literally having the Andy Warhol-prescribed 15 minutes of fame.

SHOOT-OUT 2005

The first FA Cup Final to be settled by a penalty shoot-out was the 2005 encounter between Arsenal and Manchester United. One hundred and twenty goalless minutes had seen United have much the better of the exchanges, but they were unable to apply the killer touch and the game went to penalties. After both sides had scored their opening kicks, Paul Scholes took a longer run-up than most to fire low and hard to Jens Lehmann's right. The German stopper guessed correctly and palmed out Scholes's effort and, when every other kick was converted, Arsenal became the first side to win the cup on a shoot-out with skipper Patrick Vieira scoring the match-winning penalty.

WYCOMBE CUP HERO OF 2001 ROY ESSANDOH

HOME FROM HOME 2

The Cup Final at Wembley is now a long-standing tradition, but the competition has enjoyed many different homes over the years.

1915 Old Trafford – The only wartime final saw Sheffield United beat Chelsea. Sometimes called the "Khaki Cup Final", on account of the number of uniformed soldiers in the crowd, the fact the match was played at all was controversial. Many people voiced disquiet over the continuance of professional football, while the country's youth were fighting and dying in the trenches of Europe. Poignantly, on Cup Final day itself, poisonous gas killed many young British men in Ypres.

1920-1922 Stamford Bridge – With Crystal Palace having been used as a service depot during the war and not ready to stage matches, Chelsea's home was the largest available for the first post-war finals. Luckily for the FA, Chelsea lost the 1920 semi-final to Aston Villa, and therefore avoided reaching a final which would have been played on their own ground – which would have been against the competition's rules.

1923-2000 Wembley – The Empire Stadium, as it was originally known, was built in a startling 300 days and was, by some distance, the finest football stadium in the country. Wembley was renowned for its twin towers and 39 steps up to the Royal Box, each an immovable part of Cup Final tradition. As audiences of television broadcasts increased in numbers, the ground grew in the nation's consciousness; everyone knew it, every fan wanted to go there and every footballer wanted to play there. Towards the end of its time as England's premier stadium, the original Wembley was beginning to suffer in comparison with newer stadia across the world. By the time its demise was announced, while sentimentalists lamented the loss of the twin towers, regular visitors looked forward to better views and increased leg-room.

1970 replay Old Trafford – Chelsea's first cup triumph was achieved in the mud in a match that set the benchmark for the physical battles of the 1970s.

2001-2006 Millennium Stadium – The Cardiff venue, with its steep, roomy stands and a retractable roof, set the standard for state-of-the-art stadia at the end of the 20th century. It held six finals, bookended by Liverpool wins in the first and last.

2007- (New) Wembley – With the twin towers consigned to history, the new Wembley has its own iconic feature – its spectacular arch can be seen from miles away and announces a stadium of great comfort and prestige.

STYLE OVER SUBSTANCE

The names on the Liverpool team-sheet for the 1996 FA Cup Final against Manchester United were impressive: agile keeper David James, stylish wide-man Steve McManaman, the still influential John Barnes, a powerful Stan Collymore, an aging Ian Rush and, in Robbie Fowler, a striker fast approaching his fantastic pomp. Although it was undoubtedly a team with style, sadly for Liverpool fans, it did not prove to be a team of great substance. That Liverpool team won plaudits for some fine individual performances and occasional stylish performances, but other than a solitary League Cup Final win over second tier Bolton Wanderers in 1995, they won little else. A suspicion lurked that Roy Evans's Liverpool flattered to deceive and was some way short of being the real deal their supporters had enjoyed cheering on for close to three decades of unparalleled success. Players, teams and even clubs can get stuck with labels that can be hard to shake off and this happened to the mid-1990s Liverpool vintage. The "Spice Boys" tag became applied to Evans's men at every opportunity by some press reporters; it characterised many of the squad as more interested in fame, grooming, money and even modelling for Armani than in matters on the pitch. Whether that was true or not, impressions count for a lot, and the impressions Liverpool made in their pre-match stroll around Wembley before the 1996 Cup Final were not good. The sober dark suits, perhaps garnished with a spray of carnations, favoured by most footballers over the decades for their pre-match ruminations, were eschewed. Instead, inspired allegedly by part-time Armani model and sometime top-class goalkeeper James, Liverpool opted to be daring in their attire. They strolled around the Wembley pitch bedecked in some very striking cream Armani suits, paired with light blue shirts, complemented with red and white striped ties. Luminaries such as Jamie Redknapp and the dropped Neil Ruddock decided to add further relish to the sartorial pudding by donning designer sunglasses on a day that was short of sunshine. However much time and energy had gone into their pre-match gear, Liverpool's insipid performance left their fans wishing as much attention to detail had gone into their actual game-plan. The Spice Boys barely mustered an effort on goal in 90 minutes between them, before losing to a solitary strike from an undisputed footballer with style – the high-collared and high-wired Eric Cantona scored the late winner.

RIPPING UP THE FORMBOOK 2

In nearly 70 years since the end of the war, only six times have non-league teams knocked top flight (First Division and Premiership) sides out of the FA Cup. Here are the remaining three occasions:

1974/75 Third round
Burnley 0 Wimbledon (Southern League) 1

For a couple of years in the mid-1970s Burnley were a respectable First Division outfit, while Wimbledon were still hoping to gain entry to the Football League. For 90 minutes at Turf Moor though, the difference in divisions and league placings counted for little as Burnley could not find a way past the Wimbledon defence. When Mick Mahon then put the Southern Leaguers ahead after the break, Wimbledon keeper Dickie Guy seemed inspired and stopped everything that came his way. Wimbledon were then drawn against league champions Leeds in the next round and continued their heroics, holding on for a 0-0 draw at Elland Road, thanks in part to a Guy penalty save. Leeds finally won the replay.

1985/86 Third round
Birmingham City 1 Altrincham (Alliance Premier League) 2

Future England number one David Seaman was on the receiving end as regular non-league giant-killers Altrincham were at it again. With the match evenly poised at 1-1, Blues' Robert Hopkins launched into a trademark tackle which only succeeded in finding his own net to send the Blues spinning out of the cup.

1988/89 Third round
Sutton United (Vauxhall Conference) 2 Coventry City 1

Cup winners just 18 months earlier, Coventry City were riding high in fourth place in the First Division when they arrived at Gander Green Lane. Sutton took a half-time lead only for Coventry to level things up shortly after the interval, before bricklayer Matthew Hanlon shook the Sky Blues to their foundations with a close-range volley. Although Sutton were taken to pieces by Norwich City 8-0 in round four, their achievement can be gauged by the fact that no top tier team has since fallen to non-league opposition.

JEEPERS KEEPERS 2

After the heroics of Bert Trautmann in the 1956 final, the next two years saw more traumas for the number ones at Wembley. When youthful champions Manchester United met Aston Villa in the 1957 final, United were favourites to complete the league and cup Double against a mid-table Villa side whose ranks included star winger Peter McParland. The Villa forward took just seven minutes to make his mark on the final, brutally shoulder-charging United keeper Ray Wood after his own header was saved. Although the challenge was considered fair and within the laws of the game back in the 1950s, it was hard enough to put Wood on a stretcher and on his way to hospital. A challenge like that in the modern era would no doubt lead to a lengthy ban, however McParland was free to play on. Wood did return to the action later in the match, first as a makeshift right-winger, and latterly back in goal, but it was an afternoon to forget for the United keeper. After taking over the goalkeeper's jersey, Jackie Blanchflower performed credibly for United, handling crosses and shots well, though he could do nothing about the two goals that Villa did score. McParland was on target with a diving header and a thumping rebound and though United pulled one back through Tommy Taylor it was Villa's day and they won a seventh FA Cup. Things did not improve much for one man in between the sticks in the 1958 final. Not quite three months after losing eight first-teamers in the tragedy of Munich, Manchester United had pulled together a team to reach their second successive final against Bolton. Probably no-one in the country outside of Bolton wanted them to win, yet it turned out to be a game too far for United as Wanderers won in straightforward fashion 2-0, with star striker Nat Lofthouse scoring both goals. Lofthouse's first was a smart poacher's finish, sliding in from six yards, but it was his second goal which remains one of Wembley's most controversial. When Harry Gregg in the United goal saved Dennis Stevens' shot, he could only push the ball high into the air inviting the Bolton number nine to challenge him. Lofthouse took up the invitation like a man possessed and simply charged into Gregg. It was less of a shoulder charge and more of an almighty whack in the back, leaving Gregg unconscious and the ball in the back of the net. Although football in the 1950s was undeniably harder and tougher than the modern game, arguments as to whether the goal should have stood or not raged. The debates were too late to help a bruised and battered Gregg, but the incident helped pave the way for the much improved protection for goalkeepers which they still enjoy.

WEMBLEY'S GREATEST UPSETS

FA Cup Final 1988: Liverpool 0 Wimbledon 1

The 1987/88 Liverpool vintage were widely regarded, even at the time, as a special team; they had won the league at a canter and given some exhilarating displays along the way. By contrast, Wimbledon were noted for some different characteristics; they were a rugged, physical outfit with an impressive team spirit, but perhaps, not much else. The stature of the clubs could not have been much further apart; just ten years before Liverpool were busy retaining the European Cup, while Wimbledon were busy enjoying their first season in the Football League. Anfield regularly packed in over 40,000 fans a game, while Plough Lane seldom topped 10,000. Even the opposing managers betrayed the chasm between the clubs. Kenny Dalglish preached free-flowing, fast incisive football as Bobby Gould exhorted more blood, more sweat and more tears. On the pitch, Liverpool were spearheaded by a magnificent attack; John Barnes and Peter Beardsley were fleet-footed forwards who created chance after chance for John Aldridge to convert with unerring accuracy. Wimbledon's charge was led by the muscular, combative John Fashanu and a busy, nuisance of a forward called Terry Gibson; they were backed up by the driving force of Vinny Jones, a bricklayer of a footballer who was about to build the foundations for an unbelievable afternoon. Liverpool started well and on 35 minutes thought they had opened the scoring when Beardsley rode an Andy Thorn challenge to slot home. Referee Hill had already blown for the foul and, much to Beardsley's chagrin, allowed no advantage to be played. Within two minutes everything changed. Lawrie Sanchez rose well to meet a Dennis Wise free kick and guide a header home; the script, it seemed, had been ripped up and forgotten. Liverpool pressed for an equaliser and on the hour they were awarded a penalty for Goodyear's foul on Beardsley. Aldridge had scored 11 penalties that season, but that counted for nothing as Dave Beasant threw himself to his left to push away the ball and become the first goalkeeper to save a penalty in a Cup Final. As the final whistle approached Liverpool pressed and pressed, but Wimbledon, as underdogs often have, sensed victory and simply clung on. John Motson famously declared that "the Crazy Gang have beaten the Culture Club" and he had a point. In a season of some sumptuous attacking football, Liverpool's artists has somehow been undone by Wimbledon's artisans, and the glorious unpredictability of the FA Cup was there for all to see.

THE SEAGULLS HAVE LANDED

The early 1980s were a funny time. A lot of people seemed to like a lot of attention; shoulder pads were in; big hair was in; amazingly, mullets were in too. Football was not immune from the high-impact gesture which screamed out "look at me!" as we saw when Brighton and Hove Albion reached their first FA Cup Final in 1983, to play Manchester United. The Seagulls landed at Wembley after enduring a miserable league season which saw them relegated from the First Division after just four years in the top flight. Albion's cup form, though, had been excellent throughout, defeating Newcastle United, Manchester City and famously even knocking out Liverpool at Anfield. Still, they were not expected to beat a strong United side littered with star names. As excitement in Brighton rose, temporary manager Jimmy Melia revelled in the increased media spotlight and his white shoes became as well known as skipper Steve Foster's trademark headband. The talking points were not just sartorial however, as someone, somewhere decided the team bus should be swopped for a ride in one of the helicopters owned by club sponsors British Caledonian; win or lose, Albion were certainly going to be noticed. For the first time in FA Cup Final history a team flew to Wembley by helicopter, thereby guaranteeing a blizzard of publicity. Despite Albion touching down at a school close to Wembley to drive the rest of the way, headline writers up and down the country warmed to the task of penning the best aviation puns they could muster. Legend has it though, that the line of the day, upon landing, came not from any quick-witted journalist, but from the pilot who echoed Neil Armstrong's Apollo 11 trip with the memorable line: "The Seagulls have landed!" Sadly for Albion fans the pre-match ride did not quite do the trick as they were held to a 2-2 draw before receiving a 4-0 thumping in the replay. Of course, had striker Gordon Smith converted a fantastic chance moments from the end of extra time in the first match, perhaps Brighton could have established a new superstition of flying around Wembley with the cup!

CONTINENTAL DRIFT

In the first 125 years of FA Cup competition no foreign coach or manager ever led a team to an FA Cup victory. When Ruud Gullit became the first manager of an FA Cup winning team who was not British, back in 1997 with Chelsea, it looks like, not for the first time, the Dutchman started a trend. In the last 16 seasons, foreign coaches have triumphed in England's premier domestic cup competition no less than 13 times. This dramatic

THE MOST FAMOUS CUP FINAL MISS: BRIGHTON'S GORDON SMITH IS DENIED A WINNING GOAL BY GARY BAILEY

change in emphasis reflects the much less parochial nature of English football and points to the now well-established cosmopolitan make-up of the modern game. This trend is best seen at Stamford Bridge where, in that 16-year period, Chelsea have won an astonishing six FA Cups, each time under a different foreign coach!

1997	Ruud Gullit from the Netherlands led Chelsea
1998	Arsene Wenger from France led Arsenal
1999	Alex Ferguson from Scotland led Manchester United
2000	Gianluca Vialli from Italy led Chelsea
2001	Gérard Houllier from France led Liverpool
2002	Arsene Wenger from France led Arsenal
2003	Arsene Wenger from France led Arsenal
2004	Alex Ferguson from Scotland led Manchester United
2005	Arsene Wenger from France led Arsenal
2006	Rafael Benítez from Spain led Liverpool
2007	José Mourinho from Portugal led Chelsea
2008	Harry Redknapp from England led Portsmouth
2009	Guus Hiddink from the Netherlands led Chelsea
2010	Carlo Ancelotti from Italy led Chelsea
2011	Roberto Mancini from Italy led Manchester City
2012	Roberto Di Matteo from Italy led Chelsea

ICONIC GOALS – KEITH HOUCHEN

In the summer of 1986 Keith Houchen was an unremarkable striker for unremarkable Fourth Division outfit, Scunthorpe United. Houchen had only been at the club a couple of months and like his team, who finished 15th, he had not enjoyed a vintage season. Almost 18 months earlier Houchen had enjoyed fleeting fame as the scorer of an FA Cup penalty winner against Arsenal, but his headline-making days seemed to have stalled. When that year's FA Cup Final was broadcast between Everton and Liverpool, Houchen watched the game in the Newport & District Working Men's Club in Middlesbrough as the Reds clinched the Double at the expense of their Merseyside rivals, never imagining that just 12 months later he would go on to play a starring role in another Wembley drama. First Division Coventry City showed interest in Houchen that summer, and his decision to move to Highfield Road was straightforward. Leaving behind the lower leagues and going up three divisions to Coventry was just the sort of opening Houchen had been waiting for; it was a chance to see if he could play at the top level, against the best players in the country. Though Coventry had been in the First Division for 20 successive years, they were not high-flyers; in fact they had carved out a niche for themselves as perennial relegation-fighters. However, under the wily leadership of John Sillett and George Curtis, the 1986/87 season was to be different; Coventry stayed in the top half of the table and began a thrilling cup run. Houchen scored decisive goals against Manchester United and Sheffield Wednesday in the fourth and sixth rounds of the FA Cup and followed them up with another strike in the semi-final against Leeds United, a thriller which Coventry won 3-2. By the time the final arrived, Houchen was becoming less of a journeyman striker and more of a Roy of the Rovers figure. Tottenham Hotspur faced Coventry in the final and the Londoners were highly fancied; their team was bursting with major talents like Hoddle, Waddle and Ardiles, and with an hour gone, Spurs led a close match 2-1. Coventry though were very much in the contest when goalkeeper Ogrizovic launched a long ball on to the head of Cyrille Regis. Houchen collected Regis's flick; he instantly controlled and laid the ball off to winger Dave Bennett. Smart, deft touches from Bennett allowed him to swiftly deliver a cross; the ball swung away from the goalkeeper, in between defenders and on to the six-yard line. Like a smiling assassin, Houchen anticipated better than everyone else and got ready for his kill; he leapt full-length to meet the perfect cross with the perfect, flying header. Coventry went on to win the match 3-2, and claimed the cup for the first time. Houchen's header instantly entered FA Cup folklore as one of the best cup final goals, as sublime as it was spectacular.

BRONZE IS BEST

Before semi-finals were played at Wembley, there was a common idea that losing in the semi-final was the worst stage of the competition to lost at. The logic was, that even if you reached the final and lost, at least you would have enjoyed the great day out at Wembley. Traditionally, losing semi-finalists had nothing to show for their efforts, but that was turned on its head in 1970 when a third/fourth place play-off was introduced. Apart from perhaps becoming a money-spinner for the clubs involved, the idea was to promote the idea that finishing third was a desirable thing in itself. Convincing the public that it wasn't a pointless match for losers was another story. The first match, in April 1970, saw Manchester United play

Watford; United had narrowly lost out in a second replay to Leeds United while the Hornets had been thrashed 5-1 by Chelsea. It is fair to say the fixture did not catch the public's imagination as just over 15,000 attended Highbury, the designated neutral venue. Things did not improve much over the next four years either, with continued low crowds reflecting the public apathy. Although the FA tinkered with the format of the match, changing it from an end-of-season affair to a curtain-raiser for the new season, the writing was on the wall for the occasion. People simply did not take to a fixture you could only qualify for by losing out on appearing in a Cup Final and after five attempts, this poor man's Charity Shield was consigned to the history books. Following United's victory over Watford, Stoke City beat Everton 3-2 in 1971, Birmingham City won 4-3 on penalties after a 0-0 draw against Stoke a year later – the first FA Cup tie ever settled on penalties – then Wolverhampton Wanderers beat Arsenal 3-1 in 1973, and the last match in 1974, attended by less than 6,500 supporters, saw Burnley beat Leicester City 1-0.

NUMBER CRUNCHING 3

6: During their successful FA Cup campaign in the 1947/48 season, Manchester United played against six First Division teams on their way to Wembley. It remains the only time a team has won the cup by playing top flight teams in every round.

5.15pm: The traditional kick-off time for the FA Cup Final was changed from 3pm to 5.15pm in 2012. The move by the FA was a bid to help them maximise television viewing figures, both domestically and internationally. The change was not popular with Liverpool fans who were due to attend the match though, as it coincided with long-planned maintenance work, leaving many without a route home.

4: The most number of times a team has reached the FA Cup Final and never won the competition. This unwanted honour belongs to Leicester City who contested, and lost in 1949 to Wolves, in 1961 to Tottenham, in 1963 to Manchester United and in 1969 to Manchester City.

0: In answer to the quiz question: "What is taken to Wembley every year and never used?" 0 is the number of times the loser's ribbons have been used at Wembley!

AN EVENING CELEBRATION: CHELSEA WON THE FIRST FINAL TO KICK OFF AT 5.15PM

THE BIG GIRL'S BLOUSE

Conference side Stevenage Borough drew Newcastle United in the fourth round of the 1998 FA Cup and before even a ball was kicked the tie became steeped in controversy. When the draw was made, Premiership Newcastle were due to visit non-league Stevenage's humble Broadhall Way home for an archetypal third round affair between underdog and top dog; it was the sort of pairing that keeps football romantics in business. In the build-up to the match however, there was little sweet talk from either outfit as Newcastle made noises about the unsuitability of Stevenage's ground. When United offered to switch the match to their own St James' Park, their intent was benevolent, but fans across the nation railed against the Magpies' perceived arrogance; like a Hollywood star, they were, it seemed, too big to play on the small stage. The furore reached fever pitch when the serious current affairs show *Newsnight* sought to get to the bottom of the matter by letting loose Jeremy Paxman on Newcastle boss Kenny Dalglish. The gnarled inquisitor took on the gritted-teeth manager and, in a brilliant display of how to reach the nation's zeitgeist, simply asked Dalglish if, by seeking to move the tie away from Broadhall Way, he wasn't just being a "big girl's blouse". While Dalglish had almost definitely heard every conceivable football-related question many, many times over, Paxman's angle was the verbal equivalent of facing Bobby Gould's Wimbledon; it was direct, disrespectful and in your face. The taciturn Scot was not impressed. Stevenage, of course, refused to switch venues and, after the row which preceded it, the tie was in danger of becoming a simple footnote in FA Cup history. Thankfully, there was almost as much drama to come on the field as off it. Alan Shearer headed home an early opener only for Stevenage's Giuliano Grazioli to level before the interval. No further goals were added which meant that Newcastle's hopes of hosting the non-leaguers would eventually be realised as, purely on merit, Stevenage had earned a second attempt at pulling off an almighty shock. United narrowly won the replay 2-1 and went on to reach the final at Wembley that year. Stevenage earned both plenty of gate money and, maybe even more importantly, the respect of the nation for refusing to bow to their Premiership opponents' wishes; that they should give up their home advantage and the chance of an upset in front of their own fans.

ICONIC GOALS – RONNIE RADFORD

The third round has long enjoyed a wonderful habit of pitching together teams and clubs of huge contrasts. In February 1972, at Edgar Street, football romantics would have relished six-time cup winners Newcastle United of the First Division visiting Southern League outfit Hereford United. It was a quintessential FA Cup tie; underdogs desperate to cause an upset; elite footballers desperate to avoid an embarrassment. Though in terms of status there was much to separate the teams, by the time Newcastle arrived the sides had already shared four goals in the first match, leading to a replay. Despite Hereford's heroics at St James' Park, the presumption was that their chance of an upset had passed; United's team, including the rapidly emerging Malcolm Macdonald, would surely not get caught napping a second time. However, despite much Newcastle pressure the match was goalless until the 82nd minute when Macdonald rose at the far post to nod Newcastle side ahead. The striker's clenched fist indicated the form book was back in business, while all Hereford had to do was lie down and accept their fate. Soon though one of the FA Cup's most memorable strikes was about to be unleashed. After nearly 90 minutes, Hereford's ploughed-up pitch looked less like a football field and more like a farmer's, but the non-leaguers continued to press and chase everything. When Newcastle tried to clear down their right, substitute Ricky George smartly pinched possession back to allow Ken Mallender to hoist another hopeful cross in. Once again, Newcastle's defence stood firm and the ball was cleared towards the centre circle where Ronnie Radford slipped in the mud as he won the ball. Radford looked forward and played a simple one-two with striker Brian Owen before racing on to the ball and hitting the shot of his life. Like a plane rising from a runway, the ball arrowed upwards and unstoppably, before homing in on the top-right corner of Willie McFaul's net. Radford was inspired; Hereford were level and the Bulls could smell a killing. Hereford completed a first non-league triumph over a First Division team for more than 20 years as they won 2-1 in extra time. The much repeated scenes from the *Match of the Day* cameras have since gone on to become standard-bearers for the romance of the cup. The ingredients were all in place: the battered mud-heap of a pitch; the visiting aristocrats; the hole-in-one moment of inspiration from Ronnie Radford – the magic of the cup all rolled into one glorious ball of unpredictability.

HILLSBOROUGH

On 15th April 1989, Nottingham Forest and Liverpool met in the FA Cup semi-final. Instead of the great footballing occasion it should have been remembered for, the day will only ever be known for the tragic events that led to 96 football fans losing their lives. The bare facts of the afternoon are simple: for the second successive year Liverpool and Forest were to meet in a semi-final at Hillsborough, in front of over 50,000 fans. The previous year when Liverpool had won 2-1, their fans had filled the larger end of the ground, the enormous Kop, and the game had passed without incident. Twelve months later things were different. For the 1989 match, the larger Liverpool support was given the smaller Leppings Lane end to fill. The congregating crowds were not effectively cordoned into waiting lines outside the stadium, and, fearful of a crush outside the ground, the police opened the stadium gates. This fateful decision allowed a mass of Liverpool fans into the terrace where poor signposting led hundreds of fans, anxious not to miss the start, into an already full central pen. Although the terrace behind the Liverpool goal was divided into three areas, and the left and right ones were not full, once too many fans went into the central area a dreadful, life-sapping crush developed. Just six minutes after kick-off the game was halted as it became clear that there was a major problem. The issue was exacerbated by the security fences which fringed the terraces; their presence meant the very fans who were being crushed had no means of escape. Eventually, the lives of 96 Liverpool fans were ended as a result of that afternoon. To fans of more recent times, Hillsborough can be hard to fathom; in 1989 though it was the norm for fans to watch from behind fences and for terraces to be divided into pens. Football fans were treated at best as a problem, and at worst, as animals. This attitude of herding the hordes fitted with the times; conditions for watching top-class football were uncomfortable and crowded, akin to how livestock were kept in a farmer's field. As a result, the authorities were forced to face up to football's inadequacies. As FA chairman Graham Kelly succinctly put it: "Things have to change." When the Taylor Report investigated the disaster it led to seismic changes in the national game; most pivotally, terraces were to be outlawed in favour of more sanitised, all-seated stadia. At long last, football's squalid conditions were to be consigned to the history books.

A SEA OF SCARVES AND FLOWERS IN TRIBUTE TO THOSE FANS WHO DIED IN THE FA CUP'S MOST TERRIBLE TRAGEDY

WEMBLEY'S GREATEST UPSETS

FA Cup Final 1973: Leeds United 0 Sunderland 1

The Leeds United team of 1973 had an impressive record which, before the match, appeared to dwarf the achievements of opponents Sunderland. Though the Second Division side had performed fantastically well in reaching Wembley, knocking out Manchester City and Arsenal, it was widely thought that they had reached their limits, while Leeds, it sometimes seemed in the early 1970s, had no limits at all. The Elland Road men were defending FA Cup holders, they were in the final of the European Cup Winners' Cup and they had just finished third in the league, whereas Sunderland had done well since Christmas to finish in the top six of the second tier. Though in boxing terms the 1973 final was Heavyweight v Lightweight, as the match unfolded it was anything but. There were no explosive, knockout moments from Leeds as Sunderland contained them for the first 30 minutes before the unthinkable happened. A Billy Hughes corner found its way to Ian Porterfield just outside the six-yard box and the midfielder calmly controlled the ball on his thigh before turning instantly to fire his shot high into the roof of David Harvey's net. Leeds seemed stunned by the blow, but after half-time they came out with a renewed purpose, piling on the pressure. After little more than an hour, United thought they had done enough to equalise. Right-back Paul Reaney crossed to the onrushing left-back Trevor Cherry, his contact was good and he headed far to Jim Montgomery's left. The Sunderland number one dived to save the header with both hands only for it to fall into the path of the onrushing Peter Lorimer. The Scottish international reputedly had the hardest shot in football at the time; if he hit a ball, it stayed hit. Lorimer seized his chance to level; he connected perfectly as he belted the rebounding ball back at Montgomery's unguarded goal. A prostrate Montgomery sprang up, like an Olympic gymnast, somehow raising himself off the ground to turn Lorimer's rocket on to the crossbar. Some critics harshly pointed to an extraordinary miss, while others declared the double-save to perhaps be the finest to grace a Wembley final; it was scarcely believable. Leeds never got so close again and as the clock ticked down, the unthinkable became more and more likely. In the most sensational of FA Cup sensations, the aristocrats of Leeds were brought to their knees by the artisans of Sunderland.

ICONIC GOALS – RYAN GIGGS 1999

The sight of a bare-chested Ryan Giggs wheeling away after scoring the semi-final winner against Arsenal in 1999 has become an iconic FA Cup image. The winger's extravagant celebration fitted perfectly with a goal of the highest skill and drama. Having already played out a 0-0 draw, Manchester United and Arsenal, the top two teams of the season, had to meet once again at Villa Park. Although United went on to claim a spectacular Treble just weeks later, when the sides lined up for their replay, Arsenal were still in the hunt for a second successive league and cup Double of their own. In the match, just as in the season, there was nothing to separate the teams; Beckham nudged United ahead before Bergkamp equalised. With only a minute left of normal time United looked to be heading out; Roy Keane had been red-carded and Dennis Bergkamp had a last-minute penalty to send Arsenal through to Wembley. When keeper Peter Schmeichel memorably saved the spot-kick, 30 minutes of extra time was required. Desperate not to concede again, hoping to survive for penalties and mindful of committing too many men forward, United were on the back foot. It seemed that the Old Trafford men needed a minor miracle to survive; then, with ten minutes left, a miracle-worker called Ryan Giggs took centre-stage. An unusual misplaced pass from Patrick Vieira was collected by Giggs 15 yards inside his own half. With few attacking options in front of him, the wide-man simply set off at a hopeful gallop down the left wing; the rock-like figures of Lee Dixon, Martin Keown and Tony Adams lay between Giggs and David Seaman's goal. Giggs appeared to glide rather than run upon the grass as he accelerated first past Vieira, then beyond Dixon, before cutting inside a now scrambling Keown; the Arsenal defensive pillars were in pieces. Keeper Seaman barely had time to crouch down ready for action before a thumping drive flew past him into the roof of Arsenal's net as Giggs sent United players and fans alike into orbit. Goals can stand out for any reason; for power, for trickery or for guile, but few illuminate like Giggs's effort. He was rocket-fuelled; he was graceful; he was deadly. For the Arsenal defence the daring, fleet-footed Giggs in full flow was the ultimate nightmare, for United fans and lovers of spectacular football, Giggs' play touched heights rarely, rarely seen, as he attained a little bit of football perfection.

MATTHEWS AND MORTENSEN

For the third time in six years, Blackpool, with Stanley Matthews in their ranks, reached the final in 1953. The Seasiders had lost their first two; a 4-2 defeat against Manchester United in 1948 and three years later a 2-0 loss to Newcastle United. With Matthews seemingly entering the twilight of his career, aged 38, many neutrals hoped the undisputed star of the English game would break his and Blackpool's duck and finally receive a winner's medal. Bolton had other ideas and inside two minutes Nat Lofthouse's effort was fumbled in by Blackpool keeper George Farm. The score stayed like that for more than 30 minutes until Stan Mortensen ran purposefully down the left, outpaced the Wanderers defence and fired home. Within minutes though, Farm's difficult afternoon got worse; he committed the cardinal error of coming for, and missing, a cross, allowing Langton's centre to creep in. When Eric Bell nodded home early in the second half the cup seemed destined for Burnden Park, but it was then the comeback began. First Matthews sprinted down the right, outpacing Ralph Banks, before his cross caused confusion in the Bolton box allowing Mortensen to bundle in a second. With just two minutes left of the 90, Bolton conceded a direct free kick on the left of their penalty area, which Mortensen stood over. The ferocity with which Mortensen then hit the ball left Bolton keeper Hanson motionless; it had crashed into the net before he had time to blink, never mind move. With only injury time remaining, momentum was now with Blackpool and their talisman Matthews provided another moment of magic down the wing. A twist and a jink left Banks, who was struggling with cramp, floundering; Matthews pulled back the perfect ball through a crowd of players for Bill Perry to slot home the winning goal. With two minutes remaining the engravers might have been forgiven for etching Bolton's name on the cup. That was until the most dramatic turnaround in Cup Final history delivered the cup to Blackpool in what would become known as the "Matthews Final", despite Mortensen's hat-trick.

TOP MEN

Until being taken over by Chelsea and England left-back Ashley Cole, three men shared the record of having won the most FA Cups with five. They were Charles Wollaston (Wanderers), Arthur Kinnaird (Wanderers and Old Etonians), and Jimmy Forrest (Blackburn Rovers).

RECORD NUMBER OF MEDALS: ASHLEY COLE CELEBRATES WIN NUMBER FIVE

TRISKAIDEKAPHOBIA

An enduring appeal of the FA Cup is that the rich and glorious can be drawn against the poor and lowly in any round, in any year. When Tottenham Hotspur were paired with Crewe Alexandra in the fourth round in January 1960 it was just one of those occasions. In 1960 Bill Nicholson's Tottenham were beginning to fly. Spurs finished third that season only two points from the summit of the league, and little over 12 months later the glory team of Dave Mackay, Danny Blanchflower and Les Allen would go on to secure the first league and cup Double of the 20th century. If Tottenham were footballing aristocracy, Crewe were rooted amongst the peasantry, having spent three of the previous four years bottom of the old Third Division North. Times were difficult for Crewe and that miserable run was barely improved upon by finishing a lowly 18th in the first year of the new Fourth Division. When the teams lined up at Gresty Road, Crewe were massive underdogs. By the end of the season 79 league places would separate Crewe and Tottenham, but for 90 minutes the sides slugged out an even contest that finished 2-2. The majority of Crewe's still record attendance of 20,000 left Gresty Road delighted with the home side's efforts in securing a replay. Days later though, the gap in quality became painfully clear for all to see. Over 60,000 packed into a muddy White Hart Lane for the replay to see Spurs take Crewe apart, almost limb by limb. After their titanic efforts in the first match three days earlier, Crewe's Railwaymen simply ran out of steam and trailed 10-1 at half-time. Les Allen scored five times, Bobby Smith four and Cliff Jones three, as Crewe conceded three hat-tricks in one match. The avalanche of goals slowed a little in the second period with only three more strikes added, leaving Spurs 13-2 winners. Legend has it that as Crewe began the long trek back home, they boarded a night train in Euston on platform 13, only to get off in Crewe at platform 2. However traumatised the Crewe players might have been after their mauling, lessons had to be learnt as the two sides met up again in the fourth round the following year. While fear of the number 13 was spreading through the streets of South Cheshire, like a gentle locomotive, Crewe's team had made some slow and steady progress in 12 months, as Tottenham's winning margin was this time reduced to an almost paltry 5-1.

NO CASE FOR THE DEFENCE

When Manchester United completed an unprecedented Treble of Premiership, FA Cup and Champions League in 1999, it was hard to spot too many clouds on the Old Trafford horizon. Alex Ferguson's team had conquered all comers at home and in Europe and as the dust settled on that epic season, thoughts turned to United's defence of their titles the follow campaign. The footballing talk was soon derailed though, as stories emerged in the summer of 1999 that United were considering not defending the FA Cup. United had been asked to compete in the first Fifa World Club Championship in Brazil in January 2000 when their defence of the trophy should have started. At the time, the Fifa competition was lauded as being the start of something prestigious and enduring (although the next two scheduled events were both cancelled), and pressure on United was mounting from the FA. Rumours circulated that had the Old Trafford men not agreed to their trip to Brazil, England's bid for the 2006 World Cup would be compromised; for once that year at least, it seemed whatever they did, United could not win. The final decision to withdraw from the 1999/2000 FA Cup left a bitter taste for many. Still in the first flush of Premiership television riches, United at the time were one of the world's very richest clubs; the idea that they could not assemble enough players to compete on two fronts left many scratching their heads. Incredulous fans and commentators alike could not fathom how a 127-year-old tradition of cup winners defending their trophy was to be abandoned. The decision inadvertently dealt a massive blow to the prestige, perhaps even the integrity, of the competition, as United tried to please the FA, England's World Cup bid and their own fans all at once. The end result was a diminished competition in 2000, and, not for the last time, an unprecedented departure from FA Cup tradition.

FIRST STRIKE

The first round of the FA Cup was played on 11th November 1871 and the first recorded goal was scored by Jarvis Kenrick. He was playing for Clapham Rovers against Upton Park and scored the first in a 3-0 win. Kenrick went on to play with some distinction, winning the cup three years running with Wanderers, scoring in the 1877 and 1888 finals.

PROUD AS PUNCH

Cup holders Wolves were justifiably proud of their Wembley triumph in 1949. In fact, they were so proud that by the time the third round of the following year's competition came around, they decided to show off their trophy once more. Wolves took the cup with them to their third round tie, away at Plymouth Argyle, where it was carried around the perimeter of the pitch, on a stretcher! Whether this was an early-recorded example of gamesmanship, or just sheer enthusiasm, is difficult to gauge from the distance of so many years, but if the exhibition of the cup was meant to faze Plymouth, it didn't work, as the lowly Second Division outfit battled to a 1-1 draw before bowing out in a replay at Molineux.

LAST ORDERS FOR PLUMLEY

Watford reached the last four of the FA Cup in 1987 and hopes were high that they could go on to reach a second final in four years. For that to happen, the Hornets would need to be at their best against an in-form and talented Tottenham Hotspur team. Most pundits reckoned that Watford would need a stroke or two of good luck to upset a highly-fancied Tottenham, and it was this crucial ingredient for cup success that was about to go missing from the Vicarage Road camp. First-choice keeper Tony Coton was ruled out with a broken finger, leaving veteran Steve Sherwood to replace him. Rather than risk an 18-year-old rookie keeper called David James as a substitute, Watford needed to find a non cup-tied keeper to hopefully just sit on the bench and watch the action unfold. At the time, Eddie Plumley was Watford's chief executive and he had a goalkeeping son who had retired from the game just a year before having played over 200 games. Plumley senior's idea was to get son Gary to be the spare custodian who would hopefully not be used anyway. Gary Plumley was working in a restaurant in Newport when he took a call from his father, outlining Watford's predicament. All Gary had to do was go and train for a few days, enjoy the best seat in the house for the semi-final and then go back to serving his customers. The plan could not be simpler, what could go wrong? When Steve Sherwood dislocated a finger in training in the week before the semi-final, Plumley was suddenly thrust into the limelight – he had to play. From keeping his customers happy to keeping Hoddle and Waddle at bay was a dramatic change in Plumley's working week; Watford fans held their collective breath hoping that Plumley would hold his nerve. Within little over half an hour Watford trailed 3-0, their hopes of Wembley in

1996 MATCH-WINNER FOR MANCHESTER UNITED ERIC CANTONA

tatters. Plumley spilled a fierce Clive Allen shot for the first, suffered a deflection for the second and watched a Paul Allen rocket beat him at this near post for the third. Although a harsh critic might have found fault with Plumley's hands once or twice, he had played credibly in a team that were well beaten; the fairytale call-up though did not have a happy ending.

AT THE DOUBLE

There have been seven occasions when clubs have ended the season as both league champions and FA Cup winners. After Preston and Aston Villa did the Double in the earliest days of professional football, it took another 64 years for anyone to match that feat, with Bill Nicholson's stylish Tottenham repeating the trick in 1961. In more recent times, the Double has become a little more common, but it remains a mark of undisputed achievement.

1888/89 Preston North End were unbeaten in the league all season, and did not concede a single goal in five FA Cup ties.

1896/97 Aston Villa enjoyed a golden spell, winning five league championships and two FA Cups in seven years, including this Double.

1960/61 Tottenham Hotspur were renowned for their attacking flair, scoring an astonishing 115 league goals on their way to their first title for a decade and their first cup win for 40 years.

1970/71 Arsenal won their first ever Double in a memorable last week of the 1971 season. A final league victory at rivals Tottenham meant Arsenal overhauled Leeds United by a point on the Monday night and on the following Saturday, they squeezed past Liverpool 2-1 in extra time to complete the Double.

1985/86 Liverpool were led by player-manager Kenny Dalglish who scored the title-clinching goal at Stamford Bridge and then played in the final win at Wembley over local rivals Everton.

1993/94 Manchester United had waited 26 years for one league title and a year later along came another, this time alongside an FA Cup triumph. That United team played fantastic attacking football all season, culminating in a 4-0 Cup Final win over Chelsea.

1995/96 Manchester United secured their second Double in three years courtesy of Eric Cantona's Wembley winner against Liverpool. This was also the year Alan Hansen famously declared United would "win nothing with kids".

1997/98 Arsenal came from behind in the spring of 1998 to secure the top two domestic trophies. At one point, Arsenal were 12 points behind Manchester United, but the Gunners hit tremendous form and timed their charge to perfection.

1998/99 Manchester United famously became the first English club to combine league, FA Cup and Champions League triumphs in one season. United's all-conquering team played a rare brand of swashbuckling football all year long.

2001/02 Arsenal secured a third Double for the club and a second under Arsene Wenger. Days after defeating Chelsea in the Cup Final, Arsenal won a pivotal game at Old Trafford to add the title as well.

2009/10 Chelsea won the domestic Double for the first time in their history under Carlo Ancelotti. The team inspired by Cech, Terry, Lampard and Drogba might have thought they had peaked, but just two years later they enjoyed European success.

SEMI SHOCKER 2012

When Chelsea were paired with Tottenham in last year's semi-final, fans up and down the country would have expected a close-run encounter. At half-time there was just a single Didier Drogba goal separating the sides and all to play for in the second period. Minutes after the interval, Chelsea were attacking with a Frank Lampard corner which was only half-cleared to Juan Mata. He fired goalwards only to hit a melee of bodies close to the Tottenham line. The ball was heading towards the net, but simply never got there, instead crashing into the heap of bodies. Unhappily for Spurs a goal was awarded and the whole complexion of the tie was altered. Spurs then had to open up to try and get back in the game, which left them more open at the back for Chelsea to expertly exploit as they ran out 5-1 winners. The game once again strengthened the case for goal-line technology, which now seems almost inevitable.

REVENGE AT LAST

To celebrate the 140th year since the first FA Cup Final took place, a rematch between the two original finalists, Wanderers and Royal Engineers, was staged in November 2012. The sides met up again at the Surrey Cricket Club's Kennington Oval, having enjoyed some very mixed fortunes in the intervening years. While Royal Engineers have maintained a team throughout nearly a century and a half, the first winners, Wanderers, folded in the 1880s only to be reformed three years ago. If they are to return to former glories, there is plenty of hard work ahead for Wanderers, who now play in the Surrey South Eastern Combination league, 16 divisions below the Premiership. It proved a night of revenge for the Engineers who emphatically reversed the outcome of that first final with a 7-1 win. Interestingly enough, at the end of the match the original trophy was presented, courtesy of West Ham chairman David Gold, who bought the trophy outright for not far short of half a million pounds. Quite what the original players would have made of the surroundings at The Oval is anyone's guess, but with floodlights, television cameras, shirt numbers and even crossbars present, it would surely have looked like a whole new ball game.

THE CUP DRAW

For fans of all clubs there is a genuine thrill in following the FA Cup draw. The lack of any seeded teams means anyone can face anyone, and sometimes anyone can beat anyone. The draws that we have seen in recent years though are some distance from how things used to be done. Nowadays the draw is a televisual feast; in a brightly-lit studio, showcasing the new Wembley stadium, famous faces, though not necessarily famous for footballing reasons (musicians Noel Gallagher and Serge Pizzorno from Kasabian once drew out the teams) will chuckle their way through the draw like contestants in a game show. Before the draw was ever televised, workers, schoolboys and truants alike used to huddle around transistor radios, eagerly anticipating the moment of revelation. Visions of clunking balls and velvet bags lit up listeners' minds as, with the solemnity of a church service, the nation went live to Lancaster Gate. Whichever way the draw is made it is the glorious unpredictability of it, of being at home to Hull, or away at Arsenal, that keeps us tuning in.

PART OF THE MAGIC... THE VELVET BAG AND BALLS USED FOR EACH ROUND'S FA CUP DRAW

THE GOAL THAT NEVER WAS

The 1977 cup semi-final between rivals Liverpool and Everton was a typically hard-fought tussle, with Liverpool twice leading, 1-0 and 2-1, only for Everton to twice level. With just moments left, Everton's Ronnie Goodlass broke away and crossed for Duncan McKenzie to flick on to Bryan Hamilton, who appeared to simply turn the ball in past Ray Clemence. For a split second it looked as though Maine Road was going to witness a memorable win for the Blue half of Merseyside, only for referee Clive Thomas to rule the goal out, citing an infringement. Hamilton, like almost everyone present in the ground, was certain his goal was good; the ball had gone in cleanly off his hip. Evertonians of a certain vintage will still talk about the trip to Wembley they were denied by one of the most controversial and baffling refereeing decisions in FA Cup history.

DESPERATE DAN

The 1927 final between Arsenal and Cardiff is remembered for many things; it was the first to be broadcast on the radio, the first at which *Abide With Me* was sung and, most famously of all, it was the first, and so far only, time the cup has gone out of England. Under the guidance of manager Herbert Chapman, the Arsenal team of the late 1920s was on the up. After some years of struggle in the bottom half of the First Division, Arsenal were beginning to re-emerge under Chapman's shrewd leadership, finishing second in 1926 and reaching their first Cup Final the following year. By contrast, Arsenal's opponents that day, Cardiff, seemed to be coming out of a strong period – having finished league runners-up three years earlier and been cup runners-up two years before, City had just endured a second bottom-half finish in the First Division. Match reports point to a low-key final with neither team in command for long. In the 73rd minute though, the dullness turned to drama, when Cardiff won a throw on the left. The ball found its way to the edge of the penalty area where prolific Cardiff striker Hughie Ferguson shot hard, but straight at Dan Lewis. Most times, the effort on goal would have been comfortably saved by any keeper; this time however, despite getting his hands on the ball, Arsenal's stopper somehow let it squirm under his body. As Lewis turned in desperation to retrieve it, the ball rolled into the net and in that split second, the cup was lost for Arsenal and won for Cardiff. Welshman Lewis went on to blame his fumble on a slippery new shirt which meant his grip was not secure. Indeed legend has it that his disaster spawned years of extra washes for Arsenal goalkeeping jerseys in a bid to prevent the fumble being repeated. How many extra spins and rinses the luminous modern jerseys still get is difficult to gauge, but what is certain is that for the one and, so far only time, the cup was heading out of England, thanks to one Welshman's slippery shirt.

THE PROFESSIONALS

After Upton Park and Preston drew their fourth round tie 1-1 in 1884, controversy was in the air. Upton Park were aware that Preston had included some paid players in their team and that, at the time, was against FA rules. Their complaint was upheld and Preston were thrown out of the cup so Upton Park went through to the next round. The row about paid players went far beyond one match. If anybody was in any doubt, Preston secretary William Suddell made things clear when he stated that he had indeed paid his players, as had many other clubs too. For a game that had started as an organised, amateur pursuit, this was a critical and defining moment. The fledgling football of the day was facing a potential split into two camps; those who wanted to retain amateur status, and those who did not. Within less than two years though, the matter was resolved; perhaps inevitably, the payment of players became allowed and the dawn of professional football was about to break.

SIX OF THE BEST

In the 1903 final, Bury set a record winning margin when they beat Derby County 6-0. Just one goal up at half-time, Bury went on to bury their highly-fancied opponents with five more goals in the second period to set a record final win, which still stands more than a century later. Bury's campaign was also notable for the fact that in the five matches of their cup run, the Shakers did not concede a single goal.

HEADS UP

After Shropshire Wanderers and Sheffield drew two first round FA Cup games in the 1873/74 season, a winner was needed. As no-one at the time had given a thought to such things as penalty shoot-outs, the easiest option was to simply toss a coin and award the tie to whoever called correctly. Sheffield then went into FA Cup history as the only team, probably ever, to win a tie in the competition on the toss of a coin.

HAVE WE MET BEFORE? 3

Arsenal and Newcastle have also met three times in Cup Finals, sharing the spoils and sharing one of the competition's most controversial moments.

1932 – Arsenal 1 Newcastle United 2

When Newcastle won the 1932 Cup Final, fans were left to ponder one of the most enduring controversies in the competition's long history. As they looked for a second cup triumph in three years, Arsenal grabbed an early goal to lead 1-0, but it was Newcastle's equaliser which was to live in the memory for longest. United winger Jimmy Richardson chased what looked like a lost cause down the right flank, crossing the ball only when it appeared to be out of play. Striker Jack Allen bundled the ball home and, to Arsenal's disbelief, the goal stood. Thankfully for the referee and linesman there were no super-slow-mo replays available on rolling sports channels to highlight their error, but a famous photograph did clearly show Richardson making contact with a ball that was off the field of play. To compound Arsenal's misery further, Allen later scored the winner with a smart strike from just inside the penalty area to send the cup back up to Tyneside once again.

1952 – Arsenal 0 Newcastle United 1

Newcastle became the first club to retain the trophy since the 1880s when they completed a 1-0 victory over Arsenal. United had been goal-happy all season with 98 First Division goals scored, but for most of the match they struggled to break down a resolute Arsenal. Good fortune seemed to favour the Magpies though as an early injury to Wally Barnes reduced Arsenal to ten men, but it was only in the last ten minutes that United made their advantage count. Chilean-born striker George Robledo rose highest to nod in the winner and allow Joe Harvey to receive the cup from Winston Churchill.

1998 – Arsenal 2 Newcastle United 0

Once again Arsenal were chasing a league and cup Double in 1998 when they met Newcastle, and once again they completed the job in the Wembley sunshine. Goals from Nicolas Anelka and Marc Overmars confirmed the enormous effect Arsene Wenger was having at Highbury as he began to assemble a team to challenge Manchester United's dominance.

LEE DIXON CELEBRATES ARSENAL'S VICTORY OVER NEWCASTLE UNITED IN 1998

LIGHTNING STRIKES AGAIN!

For four years running, from 1965/66 to 1968/69, Leicester City and Manchester City drew each other in the cup. In those days both were First Division outfits, and the ties were accordingly tight. The Maine Road men won by single goals in 1965 and 1966, though Leicester prevailed after a 4-3 replay in 1968. When they teams met again in 1969, this time it was in the final at Wembley, with Manchester City's Neil Young rifling home the only goal of the game after Mike Summerbee's good work.

RAMS RUN RAGGED

Usually, when a non-league side turns over more illustrious opponents in an FA Cup tie, it is a fairly close-run thing; once in a while though, the full-timers have been known to collapse like a pack of cards, as Derby did in 1955 when Boston United visited the Baseball Ground in the second round. The Pilgrims were particularly looking forward to travelling to the Baseball Ground as they had six ex-Rams players in their ranks, including Reg Harrison who had won the cup with Derby in 1946. Over 23,000 watched on, some in despair and some in delight, as a Geoff Hazeldine hat-trick fired Boston to a spectacular 6-1 win. Boston's cup adventure ended in a 4-0 defeat away at Tottenham in the following round, but the victory at Derby remains a record away win at a league club for any non-league team in the FA Cup.

THE LONGEST SEMI

In 1980, Arsenal and Liverpool took four matches and over 450 minutes to resolve their semi-final to see who would reach Wembley. A goalless first match at Hillsborough was then followed by two 1-1 draws at Villa Park. Two weeks after Second Division side West Ham had booked their place in the final, Arsenal eventually joined them after Brian Talbot scored the only goal in the only FA Cup semi-final ever played at Coventry City's Highfield Road. Arsenal went on to play a monumental 70 games that season, reaching both the FA Cup and European Cup Winners' Cup finals. Sadly for Gunners fans, Arsenal scored in neither final and lost them both, 1-0 to West Ham and then days later on penalties against Valencia.

ON THE BOX

In the days before satellite and multi-channel television, the FA Cup Final had a special place, not just in the sporting calendar, but in the minds of the nation. In the same way that non-racing fans hold office sweepstakes and turn up dutifully at bookmakers on Grand National day, so it was with the Cup Final. People with little or no interest in the sport would make an exception for one of the few days in the year when it was possible to sit down and watch all of a domestic match live on television; the screening of the FA Cup Final was, literally, a talking point for the whole country. Times change though, and as the era of very few live matches faded and was replaced by today's multi-media, multi-platform, Sky Go generation, some things have been lost from the coverage of football, particularly on Cup Final day itself. Finals in the 1970s, 80s and into the 90s offered the punters at home a lot to feast on. Even in the days of only three terrestrial channels, coverage might start on both ITV and BBC some four hours before the game was due to kick off and go on to include an array of features. You might have gazed at the BBC screening a Cup Final version of *It's A Knockout*; you could have enjoyed *Cup Final Mastermind*; you probably did follow the intimate shots of players relaxing on their team bus to Wembley. There was a bit of everything to watch on Cup Final morning and the unique build-up, even the naff bits, all helped to increase the sense of occasion. The Cup Final was a big match, it was the climax of the season and, in the days before saturation coverage of football, it mattered to everyone, even the neutrals.

ANNUS MIRABILIS

When Tottenham Hotspur's non-leaguers won the FA Cup in 1901, they had a striker in Jimmy Brown (not the Blackburn Rovers man from the story on page 112!) who just could not stop scoring. Brown scored both goals to defeat Bury, three to help beat Preston North End and all four in the semi-final against West Bromwich Albion. In front of over 114,000 spectators Brown then netted twice in the drawn final against Sheffield United, and he went on to score the clinching third goal in a 3-1 replay victory. Brown scored 15 goals in total along the way to picking up his winner's medal in what was surely his, and Tottenham's, annus mirabilis.

THREE IN A ROW

Blackburn Rovers completed a memorable hat-trick of cup triumphs from 1884 to 1886 and were the second club to achieve the feat, emulating Wanderers a decade earlier. They were helped in no small part by the goals of striker Jimmy Brown who achieved the unique distinction of scoring in three successive finals. Famously, Brown's goal in the 1886 final, his last game for Rovers, was scored after a dribble the length of the pitch.

FA CUP FINALS

1871/72 Wanderers 1 Royal Engineers 0	Kennington Oval	2,000
1872/73 Wanderers 2 Oxford University 0	Lillie Bridge	3,000
1873/74 Oxford University 2 Royal Engineers 0	Kennington Oval	2,000
1874/75 Royal Engineers 1 Old Etonians 1	Kennington Oval	2,000
(Replay) Royal Engineers 2 Old Etonians 0	Kennington Oval	3,000
1875/76 Wanderers 1 Old Etonians 1	Kennington Oval	3,500
(Replay) Wanderers 3 Old Etonians 0	Kennington Oval	3,500
1876/77 Wanderers 2 Oxford University 1	Kennington Oval	3,000
1877/78 Wanderers 3 Royal Engineers 1	Kennington Oval	4,500
1878/79 Old Etonians 1 Clapham Rovers 0	Kennington Oval	5,000
1879/80 Clapham R 1 Oxford University 0	Kennington Oval	6,000
1880/81 Old Carthusians 3 Old Etonians 0	Kennington Oval	4,500
1881/82 Old Etonians 1 Blackburn 0	Kennington Oval	6,500
1882/83 Blackburn Olympic 2 Old Etonians 1	Kennington Oval	8,000
1883/84 Blackburn 2 Queen's Park 1	Kennington Oval	4,000
1884/85 Blackburn 2 Queen's Park 0	Kennington Oval	12,500
1885/86 Blackburn 0 West Brom 0	Kennington Oval	15,000
(Replay) Blackburn 2 West Brom 0	Racecourse Grd	12,000
1886/87 Aston Villa 2 West Brom 0	Kennington Oval	15,500
1887/88 West Brom 2 Preston NE 1	Kennington Oval	19,000
1888/89 Preston NE 3 Wolves 0	Kennington Oval	22,000
1889/90 Blackburn 6 The Wednesday 1	Kennington Oval	20,000
1890/91 Blackburn 3 Notts County 1	Kennington Oval	23,000
1891/92 West Brom 3 Aston Villa 0	Kennington Oval	25,000
1892/93 Wolves 1 Everton 0	Fallowfield	45,000
1893/94 Notts County 4 Bolton Wanderers 1	Goodison Park	37,000
1894/95 Aston Villa 1 West Brom 0	Crystal Palace	42,560
1895/96 The Wednesday 2 Wolves 1	Crystal Palace	48,836
1896/97 Aston Villa 3 Everton 2	Crystal Palace	65,891
1897/98 Nottingham Forest 3 Derby County 1	Crystal Palace	62,017
1898/99 Sheffield United 4 Derby County 1	Crystal Palace	73,833
1899/1900 Bury 4 Southampton 0	Crystal Palace	68,945
1900/01 Tottenham H 2 Sheffield United 2	Crystal Palace	110,820
(Replay) Tottenham H 3 Sheffield United 1	Burnden Park	20,470
1901/02 Sheffield United 1 Southampton 1	Crystal Palace	76,914
(Replay) Sheffield United 2 Southampton 1	Crystal Palace	33,068
1902/03 Bury 6 Derby County 0	Crystal Palace	63,102

1903/04 Man City 1 Bolton Wanderers 0	Crystal Palace	61,374
1904/05 Aston Villa 2 Newcastle United 0	Crystal Palace	101,117
1905/06 Everton 1 Newcastle United 0	Crystal Palace	75,609
1906/07 The Wednesday 2 Everton 1	Crystal Palace	84,594
1907/08 Wolves 3 Newcastle United 1	Crystal Palace	74,697
1908/09 Man United 1 Bristol City 0	Crystal Palace	71,401
1909/10 Newcastle United 1 Barnsley 1	Crystal Palace	77,747
(Replay) Newcastle United 2 Barnsley 0	Goodison Park	69,000
1910/11 Bradford City 0 Newcastle United 0	Crystal Palace	69,068
(Replay) Bradford City 1 Newcastle United 0	Old Trafford	58,000
1911/12 Barnsley 0 West Brom 0	Crystal Palace	54,556
(Replay) Barnsley 1 West Brom 0	Bramall Lane	38,555
1912/13 Aston Villa 1 Sunderland 0	Crystal Palace	20,081
1913/14 Burnley 1 Liverpool 0	Crystal Palace	72,778
1914/15 Sheffield United 3 Chelsea 0	Old Trafford	49,557
1919/20 Aston Villa 1 Huddersfield Town 0	Stamford Bridge	50,018
1920/21 Tottenham H 1 Wolv'hampton W 0	Stamford Bridge	72,805
1921/22 Huddersfield Town 1 Preston NE 0	Stamford Bridge	53,000
1922/23 Bolton Wanderers 2 West Ham 0	Wembley	126,047
1923/24 Newcastle United 2 Aston Villa 0	Wembley	91,695
1924/25 Sheffield United 1 Cardiff City 0	Wembley	91,763
1925/26 Bolton Wanderers 1 Man City 0	Wembley	91,447
1926/27 Cardiff City 1 Arsenal 0	Wembley	91,206
1927/28 Blackburn 3 Huddersfield Town 1	Wembley	92,041
1928/29 Bolton Wanderers 2 Portsmouth 0	Wembley	92,576
1929/30 Arsenal 2 Huddersfield Town 0	Wembley	92,448
1930/31 West Brom 2 Birmingham City 1	Wembley	92,406
1931/32 Newcastle United 2 Arsenal 1	Wembley	92,298
1932/33 Everton 3 Man City 0	Wembley	92,950
1933/34 Man City 2 Portsmouth 1	Wembley	93,258
1934/35 Sheffield Weds 4 West Brom 2	Wembley	93,204
1935/36 Arsenal 1 Sheffield United 0	Wembley	93,384
1936/37 Sunderland 3 Preston NE 1	Wembley	93,495
1937/38 Preston NE 1 Huddersfield T 0	Wembley	93,497
1938/39 Portsmouth 4 Wolves 1	Wembley	99,370
1945/46 Derby County 4 Charlton Athletic 1	Wembley	98,000

1946/47 Charlton Athletic 1 Burnley 0	Wembley	99,000
1947/48 Man United 4 Blackpool 2	Wembley	99,000
1948/49 Wolves 3 Leicester City 1	Wembley	99,500
1949/50 Arsenal 2 Liverpool 0	Wembley	100,000
1950/51 Newcastle United 2 Blackpool 0	Wembley	100,000
1951/52 Newcastle United 1 Arsenal 0	Wembley	100,000
1952/53 Blackpool 4 Bolton Wanderers 3	Wembley	100,000
1953/54 West Brom 3 Preston NE 2	Wembley	100,000
1954/55 Newcastle United 3 Man City 1	Wembley	100,000
1955/56 Man City 3 Birmingham City 1	Wembley	100,000
1956/57 Aston Villa 2 Man United 1	Wembley	100,000
1957/58 Bolton Wanderers 2 Man United 0	Wembley	100,000
1958/59 Nottingham Forest 2 Luton Town 1	Wembley	100,000
1959/60 Wolves 3 Blackburn 0	Wembley	100,000
1960/61 Tottenham H 2 Leicester City 0	Wembley	100,000
1961/62 Tottenham H 3 Burnley 1	Wembley	100,000
1962/63 Man United 3 Leicester City 1	Wembley	100,000
1963/64 West Ham 3 Preston NE 2	Wembley	100,000
1964/65 Liverpool 2 Leeds United 1	Wembley	100,000
1965/66 Everton 3 Sheffield Wednesday 2	Wembley	100,000
1966/67 Tottenham H 2 Chelsea 1	Wembley	100,000
1967/68 West Brom 1 Everton 0	Wembley	100,000
1968/69 Man City 1 Leicester City 0	Wembley	100,000
1969/70 Chelsea 2 Leeds United 2	Wembley	100,000
(Replay) Chelsea 2 Leeds United 1	Old Trafford	62,078
1970/71 Arsenal 2 Liverpool 1	Wembley	100,000
1971/72 Leeds United 1 Arsenal 0	Wembley	100,000
1972/73 Sunderland 1 Leeds United 0	Wembley	100,000
1973/74 Liverpool 3 Newcastle United 0	Wembley	100,000
1974/75 West Ham 2 Fulham 0	Wembley	100,000
1975/76 Southampton 1 Man United 0	Wembley	100,000
1976/77 Man United 2 Liverpool 1	Wembley	100,000
1977/78 Ipswich Town 1 Arsenal 0	Wembley	100,000
1978/79 Arsenal 3 Man United 2	Wembley	100,000
1979/80 West Ham 1 Arsenal 0	Wembley	100,000
1980/81 Tottenham H 1 Man City 1	Wembley	100,000
(Replay) Tottenham H 3 Man City 2	Wembley	92,000
1981/82 Tottenham H 1 QPR 1	Wembley	100,000

(Replay) Tottenham H 1 QPR 0	Wembley	90,000
1982/83 Man United 2 Brighton 2	Wembley	100,000
(Replay) Man United 4 Brighton 0	Wembley	100,000
1983/84 Everton 2 Watford 0	Wembley	100,000
1984/85 Man United 1 Everton 0	Wembley	100,000
1985/86 Liverpool 3 Everton 1	Wembley	98,000
1986/87 Coventry City 3 Tottenham H 2	Wembley	98,000
1987/88 Wimbledon 1 Liverpool 0	Wembley	98,203
1988/89 Liverpool 3 Everton 2	Wembley	82,500
1989/90 Man United 3 Crystal Palace 3	Wembley	80,000
(Replay) Man United 1 Crystal Palace 0	Wembley	80,000
1990/91 Tottenham H 2 Nottingham F 1	Wembley	80,000
1991/92 Liverpool 2 Sunderland 0	Wembley	80,000
1992/93 Arsenal 1 Sheffield Wednesday 1	Wembley	79,347
(Replay) Arsenal 2 Sheffield Wednesday 1	Wembley	62,267
1993/94 Man United 4 Chelsea 0	Wembley	79,634
1994/95 Everton 1 Man United 0	Wembley	79,592
1995/96 Man United 1 Liverpool 0	Wembley	79,007
1996/97 Chelsea 2 Middlesbrough 0	Wembley	79,160
1997/98 Arsenal 2 Newcastle United 0	Wembley	79,183
1998/99 Man United 2 Newcastle United 0	Wembley	79,101
1999/2000 Chelsea 1 Aston Villa 0	Wembley	78,217
2000/01 Liverpool 2 Arsenal 1	Millennium	72,500
2001/02 Arsenal 2 Chelsea 0	Millennium	73,963
2002/03 Arsenal 1 Southampton 0	Millennium	73,726
2003/04 Man United 3 Millwall 0	Millennium	71,350
2004/05 Arsenal 0 Man United 0	Millennium	71,876
Arsenal won 5-4 on penalties		
2005/06 Liverpool 3 West Ham 3	Millennium	71,140
Liverpool won 3-1 on penalties.		
2006/07 Chelsea 1 Man United 0	Wembley	89,826
2007/08 Portsmouth 1 Cardiff City 0	Wembley	89,874
2008/09 Chelsea 2 Everton 1	Wembley	89,391
2009/10 Chelsea 1 Portsmouth 0	Wembley	88,335
2010/11 Man City 1 Stoke City 0	Wembley	88,643
2011/12 Chelsea 2 Liverpool 1	Wembley	89,102

FA CUP FINAL APPEARANCES

	Wins	*RU*
Manchester United	11	7
Arsenal	10	7
Tottenham Hotspur	8	1
Liverpool	7	7
Chelsea	7	4
Aston Villa	7	3
Newcastle United	6	7
Blackburn Rovers	6	2
Everton	5	8
West Bromwich Albion	5	5
Manchester City	5	4
Wanderers	5	0
Wolverhampton Wanderers	4	4
Bolton Wanderers	4	3
Sheffield United	4	2
Sheffield Wednesday	3	3
West Ham United	3	2
Old Etonians	2	6
Preston North End	2	5
Portsmouth	2	3
Sunderland	2	2
Nottingham Forest	2	1
Bury	2	0
Huddersfield Town	1	4
Southampton	1	3
Leeds United	1	3
Derby County	1	3
Royal Engineers	1	3
Oxford University	1	3
Blackpool	1	2
Cardiff City	1	2
Burnley	1	2
Charlton Athletic	1	1
Barnsley	1	1
Notts County	1	1

Clapham Rovers	1	1
Wimbledon	1	0
Coventry City	1	0
Ipswich Town	1	0
Bradford City	1	0
Blackburn Olympic	1	0
Old Carthusians	1	0
Leicester City	0	4
Birmingham City	0	2
Queen's Park	0	2
Stoke City	0	1
Millwall	0	1
Middlesbrough	0	1
Crystal Palace	0	1
Watford	0	1
Brighton & Hove Albion	0	1
Queens Park Rangers	0	1
Fulham	0	1
Luton Town	0	1
Bristol City	0	1